OUTBACK WOMEN

for mama and matie

OUTBACK WOMEN

MELISSA McCORD

TEXT BY MELISSA McCORD AND HELEN TOWNSEND

DOUBLEDAY
SYDNEY & AUCKLAND

OUTBACK WOMEN

First published in 1986 by Doubleday Australia
Pty Limited, 91 Mars Road, Lane Cove, NSW 2066

National Library of Australia
Cataloguing in Publication data

McCord, Melissa.
   Outback women.
   Includes index.
   ISBN 0 86824 248 9.

   1. Frontier and pioneer life — Australia. 2. Rural
   women — Australia. 3. Ranchers' wives — Australia. I.
   Townsend, Helen. II. Title.
994.06'3

Designed by Pam Brewster
Maps by Diana Wells

Typeset in Garamond by Graphicraft Typesetters Ltd., Hong Kong
Printed in Hong Kong by Mandarin Offset Marketing (H.K.) Ltd.

CONTENTS

ACKNOWLEDGEMENTS

The author would like to thank the following for their help on *Outback Women*:

Jonathan Throsby for initiating the trip and teaching me the art of travel, and for his patience and inspiration; all of my wonderful family and friends; the late Dr Anthony McNicholl and Tamara Winikoff for parting with their precious 'La Python'; Ross Campbell Jones for his unfailing support from beginning to end; to all those along the way who took me into their homes, were warm and kind and who made it all seem feasible; the Australian Broadcasting Commission and in particular Bernice Daly for her sensitive treatment of 'Two Women'; Dame Mary Durack for honouring me with her Foreword; Rapport Photo Agency, especially Rob Walls, Margaret Olah and Simon Cowling; Fairfax, Syme, Weldon Associates; The Royal Flying Doctor Service, the CWA, the School of the Air and shire councils who were invaluable in helping me find (and communicate with) my subjects; Helen Townsend for her infectious enthusiasm (right when I needed it) and her handling of the transcriptions; Tim Curnow and Barbara Mobbs; Jonny Lewis for his portraits.

FOREWORD

A good deal has been written of the pioneer women who braved life in the outback before the days of made roads, modern communication, transport and other facilities. It is generally accepted that their lot was considerably harder and more demanding than that of their counterparts today. This was no doubt the case in some respects, but many will be surprised to read of women in isolated circumstances throughout Australia who are coping with tougher demands than those encountered in the early days of settlement.

In fact, *Outback Women* which combines photographic portraits with information gathered from those concerned, provides a unique and moving insight into a little known aspect of contemporary Australian life.

We learn from Melissa McCord's Introduction something of the author's growing years on her family's station property in Queensland and of her later involvement in photography and associated activities in Australia and abroad. Her bush upbringing no doubt had much to do with her dauntless acceptance of outback conditions, including the long, lonely roads she travelled throughout the continent when preparing the material for this book.

The women she has portrayed represent an interesting cross-section of characters from different social, educational and racial backgrounds, some economically deprived, others in reasonably comfortable circumstances, and a few enjoying comparative luxury on well-established properties. All seem to share such admirable qualities as courage, initiative and resourcefulness. They also appear to exhibit a helpful community spirit especially in times of natural disaster such as bushfires, droughts and floods. Some tell of having worked with their husbands from their early married days on any job offering at the time, usually such occupations as yard-making, fencing, dam-sinking, droving and mustering. Some couples eventually took over the management of stations or acquired modest holdings of their own with roofs over their heads in place of tents and bought sheds. A number of women, especially since the introduction of award wages and social service benefits for Aboriginal workers, continue, despite their improved conditions, to help in the stock camps and with general station management. Others, either widowed or deserted, tell of having taken on jobs as shearers' cooks or station domestics to enable them to keep and educate their families.

A few of those encountered complain of missing social life and female company but for the most part they claim to prefer bush to city life and display an impressive self-sufficiency. Some speak of rearing their children to be as competent and independent as themselves, helping in the house and with outside station jobs. Most accept the constant and varied activities as a way of life they would not wish to change. As one of them, still mustering cattle in her mature years, forthrightly declares: 'It's better than rotting away in a wheelchair.'

Although the outback might be seen as predominantly a man's world, all those represented in this book continue to play a significant role in Australia's inland development.

Mary Durack
Perth

INTRODUCTION

To have had my bush childhood was a unique gift. My sense of belonging comes from four generations on the land. Land and family are almost indivisible, each complementing the other. There are good seasons, bad ones and years of drought. There is continual change, growth and development but there is always a sense of continuity. The environment is beautiful, but it is often harsh. The work is satisfying, but it is hard too and at times seems neverending.

My mother came from the city to a challenging, often lonely,bush life without the comforts and companionship she had always had. She has a strength and stamina that sparked my desire to document the lives of outback women.

Mama was always there. I remember her coming home to cook dinner and soothe babies after being flung from a bolting mare and kicked in the face on the way down. She has given her all, to work through drought, flood, fire and depression. But no matter how much she has had to endure physically, she has always retained her femininity. Being a woman has given her an inner strength and resilience as well as a particularly feminine sensitivity to her environment and the people around her. These qualities have been my inspiration.

I'd thought about making the trip to document the lives of outback women for a long time. I'd saved for it and prepared for it. But it was my companion, Jonathan Throsby, an artist, who got us up and going in January 1983. He's an avid traveller and was anxious to start working towards an exhibition. I had lived most of my life in the bush and had been the photographer on two archaeological expeditions in the Middle East but, I'd never been a Girl Guide and I wasn't really prepared for camping out Australian-style, in spite of my childhood in the bush. I painted the Land Rover's shelves pink, put in pink gingham curtains and packed a party frock as well as my bush gear. Jonathan cringed whenever he caught sight of the pink gingham in the rear vision mirror. However, I learned to put up with the heat, the dirt, not being able to wash and we eventually used the party frock to bind up the exhaust.

Perhaps that sounds a little naive, but I was serious about what I was doing. The journey took two years and I travelled more than 70,000 kilometres. I kept a diary, recording the landscape, the people, the heat that soared up past forty degrees, creating a landscape of shimmering mirages, the corrugated roads, thick with bulldust that enveloped the car in a continual cloud, or bogged us in the wet.

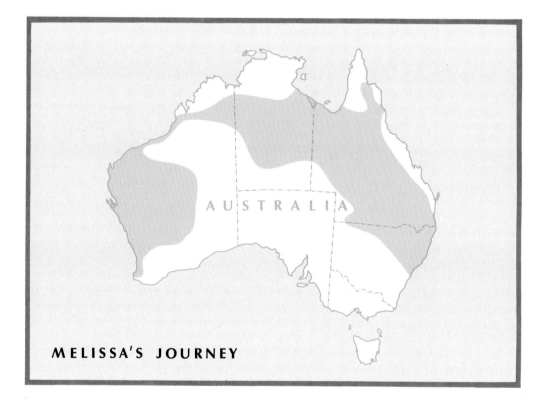

MELISSA'S JOURNEY

At first, I felt shy about approaching women to ask if I could photograph them and talk to them about their lives. Usually, they were enthusiastic about what I was doing, but couldn't see how they could be of interest. Fortunately, the actual process of photography creates a link between subject and photographer. As I set up, I'd explain what I was doing. I'd tell them why I wanted certain poses, why I wanted to emphasise certain features. They'd become involved, interested and the rapport developed. It was then easy to sit and chat with the tape recorder running.

Because the women live in such isolated circumstances, not with other people all day, not being constantly reminded of images they should live up to, they were generally unselfconscious about being photographed. They didn't insist on changing into their best frocks, putting on makeup and doing their hair. I wanted to photograph these women in their landscape. They were already very intimately involved in it, in tune with their surroundings, so even though they may not have understood exactly what I was trying to do, they weren't ill at ease. Most often, it was just the question, 'Why me?'

We had to dispose of 'La Python', as we'd christened the Land Rover, largely because of her voracious petrol consumption. We swapped her for a Peugot 403 but by Mt Isa it too was a terminal case. I sold some shares and bought a Subaru. We went up to the Gulf country to run it in, then interviewed and photographed Aboriginal women at Roper Valley Station. From there it was straight across the Northern Territory to Port Hedland. It was November, we'd been on the road almost a year, and we were broke.

For the next six months, working as a barmaid at the Esplanade Hotel, I became engrossed in the life of Port Hedland. It is a mining town, with a frontier mentality and an incredible mixture of races and characters, something I enjoyed tremendously at times and found difficult at others. One night I was pulled over the bar and bitten on the arm by a very drunk bank clerk. We experienced our first cyclone and a Yugoslav gambling joint. We got to know the locals and I took a lot of photographs and wrote up the transcripts of tapes of the women I'd already interviewed. I wrote to the Shire Councils, School of the Air, Flying Doctor and Aboriginal organisations to ask their help in finding more women. They were very obliging, but eventually I found that word of mouth was the best method.

I wasn't looking for a particular type of woman. I was looking for a cross-section — women who'd been given opportunities, women who'd created their own, women who had had good times and bad. I was looking for women with stories to tell, who had feelings and views about their lives. I found these views running through their stories, although often not consciously articulated.

Six months in Port Hedland was enough and I was anxious to complete the project. I still had the bulk of it to do, having photographed and interviewed only thirty women at this point.

I have started the book with the women of the Pilbara because it was here that the project, as a book, had really begun to take shape in my mind. It took almost another year to complete the photographs and interviews, over 100 women in all. I have arranged the book approximately following the route I took that year, moving from Western Australia, through the Territory to Queensland. But as I had already photographed and interviewed a lot of the women and because I often drove back over the same country when I heard of someone interesting, the order of the book doesn't exactly follow my travels.

Jonathan was also keen to move on but, unfortunately, in the opposite direction — back to Sydney. I was on my own and I felt a little frightened and vulnerable. But this was to be the most valuable part of the trip. For one thing, I'd been toughened up by barmaiding. I didn't have any reticence about approaching the women. I was very clear about what I wanted to do. Being alone, I was closer actually to the experience of women in isolation. It was ironic, these women would often warn me that it wasn't a good thing, a young girl alone, gallivanting around in the outback. 'Not on these roads, Melissa,' they'd say and this was from women whose isolation was extreme, who lived in the most primitive housing with almost no communication with the outside world.

I managed very well. I was not only used to camp life, I had also grown to love it. I still found much of the trip difficult and tiring. I bought a skipping rope in Port Hedland and I used to get out of the car in the middle of nowhere and skip to start the blood pumping to my brain, after hours of driving — a sort of outback aerobics.

I became more aware of what living in isolation does — the good and the bad sides. For me, one of the saddest things was what I saw happening to the Aboriginal people. I grew up with Aboriginals, who were strong, robust, proud and deeply spiritual people. My heart went out to the people in the Aboriginal settlements: their sick children, the women prostituted to itinerant workers, the men who lose everything to alcohol and drugs. I visited many camps and settlements, but one in particular sticks in my mind. I drove in late at night. There were fires everywhere, men and women lying around them, hopelessly drunk. There was continuous noise from transistors and a band screamed out over the desert. Children ran round the camp, out of control, covered in sores. Hundreds of people were living in houses that had been stripped down and virtually destroyed. It was like a scene out of a holocaust movie. It made drinking rights, equal wages and land rights seem irrelevant: white hand-outs and pay-offs have taken away the dignity of the Aboriginal people.

The Aboriginals fortunate enough not to be living in such circumstances retain their gentleness, their pride and their closeness to nature and to the land. As I travelled through the outback, I became increasingly conscious of my own dependence on the country, the weather and the seasons. It is a very different feeling from living in the city and, for the women in the outback, this close relationship to the land gives a centre to their lives. Amongst the women I talked to, there was an acceptance of life, how it is, of the often horrendous difficulties that faced them.

The isolation also means that women have a more intense relationship with their men. Sometimes they are used, discriminated against, expected to perform miracles bringing up the children and keeping the household going, as well as being involved in the outside work. But frequently, it is a partnership between man and wife, a knowledge that they really need one another. Few men and women are openly affectionate, but I often sensed a strong bond — *real* mateship.

It would be easy to romanticise all this. I met women who were desperately lonely and found it impossible to admit. Others nursed aching sorrows, feeling they could not share them, that it would be weak to do so. But in general, their closeness to nature gave them a balance within themselves, a real acceptance of life as it is, at the moment. I asked one woman whether she'd like an easier life: 'Sometimes I think it'd be all right to get a smaller place, where there's better country,' she replied thoughtfully. 'But there are other things. You know, it'd upset you. You'd be too close to town.'

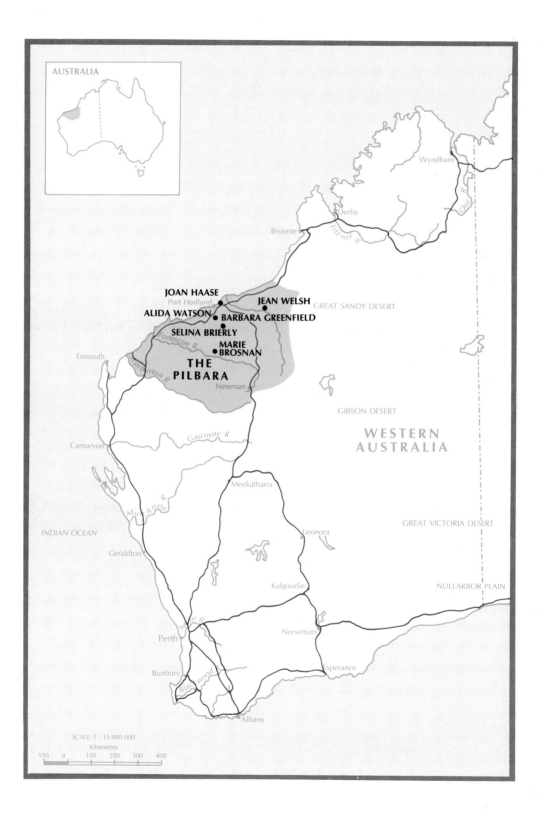

AUSTRALIA

Wyndham

Derby

Broome

JOAN HAASE
Port Hedland
JEAN WELSH GREAT SANDY DESERT
ALIDA WATSON
BARBARA GREENFIELD

Fortescue R.

SELINA BRIERLY
MARIE
BROSNAN

Exmouth

THE
PILBARA

Newman

GIBSON DESERT

Carnarvon

Gascoyne R.

WESTERN
AUSTRALIA

Meekatharra

GREAT VICTORIA DESERT

Murchison R.

INDIAN OCEAN

Leonora

Geraldton

Kalgoorlie

NULLARBOR PLAIN

Perth

Norseman

Esperance

Bunbury

Blackwood

Albany

SCALE 1 : 15 000 000
Kilometres
100   0   100   200   300   400

WOMEN OF THE PILBARA

The Pilbara is everyone's idea of the outback — rough and sparse. Any vegetation on the red, rolling hills is decidedly scrubby. Port Hedland is a sprawling, tough town, where men can make big money. A lot of it goes on drink and gambling and horse racing is an obsession. The Pilbara is a country of extremes. In summer, it is so hot that work starts very early in the morning to avoid the fierce midday sun. In winter, it can be freezing. The rains, essential for survival, are often destructive. Cyclones rip away houses and townships. What is man-made is usually temporary.

BARBARA GREENFIELD

According to the locals, Barbara Greenfield is a strong character. She lived on Tabba Tabba station all her married life. Her husband John was an invalid and Barbara had to work hard. When John died, she started up a riding school at Bosna Lodge, thirty-two kilometres from Port Hedland. She's built it up from scratch: horses, stables and yards. She got transportable houses which had been damaged in a cyclone and brought them out to the property. The whole family now lives in them. They're surrounded by pergolas, landscaped with railway sleepers and flowerbeds, all of which Barbara has built.

I married John Greenfield from Bosworth Station, Woomera, and we came up to Tabba Tabba in December, in the worst of the heat. I came up and I survived. How do you survive here? You never, ever weaken, you never give in. But I've no intention of ever living that poor or that rough again.

I had one baby that died. It was just after we'd finished the shearing. They came in the next morning and said, 'The baby's a bit cold, he went a bit blue in the night.' I rushed down to the ward. He was black, dying. John went to pieces, ravaged with depression and terribly ill. The following Sunday, a minister came out to the station to bury the baby. He came out carrying a little white cardboard box. I thought he'd brought a Christmas cake from someone. Then, I had a closer look: there was some writing on it and my baby was in there. I knew we had to have a cheap funeral, but I thought we'd at least have a coffin.

People used to come out to Tabba and feel sorry for me because I had a tin house, no air-conditioning, the babies and a sick husband. But I managed. I used to look out at the sunset and see the fractured outline of the horizon. That was my God-given time, my special time. It didn't matter what happened the next day.

I was out at Tabba for twelve years. I came into town after my husband died. I'd seen a lady in Wyandra riding along with a mob of kids behind her in the pouring rain. I thought that if she could run a riding school in the rain, I could run one in the heat. That way my kids could keep their horses. I bought a mob of ponies in Perth and mustered in all my horses from Tabba. Alida and Melissa helped me. And I got the use of this land to start the riding school.

We had kids who came from families who had even less than mine. We've had two coloured gymkhanas here. It'll grow and become a big event. There's no reason why coloureds shouldn't have their gymkhanas — whites do. It's like different churches for different people.

We live cheaply. All the food that comes into this house is a resource.

You don't turn up your nose up at horse meat. If someone brings us donkey or kangaroo, we eat it. Save money and upgrade the place. One day we had some highfalutin people come in, wanting a meal. A loaf and three fishes to feed the multitude. I told the kids to take the goanna that I'd shot down to the shed, skin it and tie its tail to its head. Stick it in the dish and don't say a word. I mixed it up with rice and fed them. Didn't tell them they were eating goanna though.

ALIDA WATSON

Alida is Barbara Greenfield's oldest daughter. She, her husband Peter and their child live in one of the cyclone damaged houses at Bosna Lodge. The riding school is very much a family affair. When Alida left home, she lived in the city and tried university and a couple of different jobs. But she is very much a country girl. She loves horses and riding and hopes to get a trainer's licence.

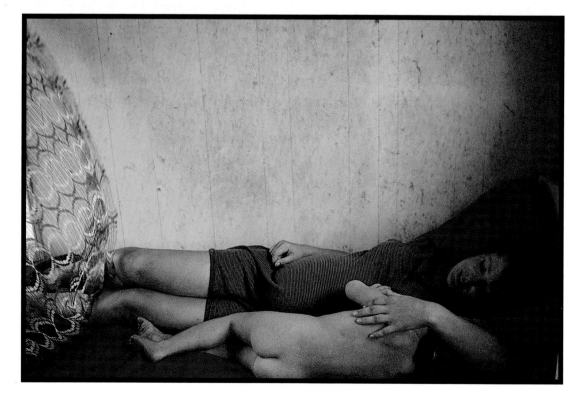

When Mum was pregnant with me, they gave her the sack, because you couldn't be pregnant, unmarried and matron of a Methodist old folks' home. She married John Greenfield, who wasn't my real father and we came to live at Tabba Tabba. I loved the station, but I left when I was seventeen — after a fight with Dad. I'd been knocking round with a young fellow who was working for us. On Christmas Eve, we were bringing the cattle in and a cow ran into this fellow's leg and cut through the shin bone. I was in charge and after we'd set up camp, I bathed his wound and we went to sleep in his swag together. Mum and Dad just happened to come out that night. Dad didn't take too kindly to me being in his swag. I left home and learned more about training horses. When Dad died, I came back here with Peter to help Mum.

Mum and I always have a good time together. One year, she suggested I do a Lady Godiva at the Spinifex Spree — that's when all the floats go round town. I made a wig from wool, plaited my horse's mane and did him up with ribbons. I changed into see-through knickers at the Ampol Depot and then rode down there while Charlie Court (a former Premier) was making the opening speech. They looked up, didn't know what to think. I was gone in a flash. It took them a while to work out who Lady Godiva was.

A few years later Mum said she reckoned the Spinifex Spree needed livening up again. I went in on Peter's horse, Rosco. He used to be a police horse. I cantered up the street once and then thought, 'Bugger it, I'm going back.' I held the wig down at first, then I got gamer and just let it go and waved to all the people, my boobs going everywhere. When I got back, there was a police car waiting. I told them I needed to get dressed. Then I went up to the station. I was fingerprinted, but they couldn't work out what to charge me with. Eventually they settled on 'disorderly conduct and careless riding'.

S ELINA BRIERLY

The Aboriginal camps outside Port Hedland present a depressing picture of drunkenness, disease and sick children. Selina Brierly's life now is a long way removed from that squalid camp living. The fact that she is married to a white man makes her unusual. The fact that the marriage is a happy, equal partnership is even more surprising.

I had a boyfriend, Captain Wilson. We worked at a couple of stations together. I used to cook or waitress for the managers, cart the tucker, that sort of stuff. Colin came along, bought this station and wanted workers. So me and Captain came and worked out here.

Captain and me used to fight a lot and that Captain, he started going round with other girls. So I just made up my mind to try and get a white man and get a nice home and settle down. The Aboriginal man, he make his wife do all the work and the men sit round and talk. I made up my mind to love Colin. We had Gail and then he asked me to get married.

I always get up early, about four or five to cook breakfast for Colin. Colin does a lot of work. I used to help him with the mustering. I used to like riding, but it makes me sore.

Sometimes we take the children out. See an emu or a kangaroo and shoot it. Pluck the emu, make a big fire, dig a hole and get some big hot rocks to go in his tummy. Then you close him up, like a chicken and steam it up inside all afternoon. I like fish best, the emu's a bit oily.

JOAN HAASE

Joan Haase is the true battler. Life has been a constant and very real struggle to survive. She has coped with situations that would defeat most people, She lives a life that by most people's standards would seem very impoverished. But she gets enormous comfort and pleasure from the animals she takes in.

I was a bush girl, the eldest of three. My father was a cripple, couldn't move around. He was six foot four, but had one leg that was only as thick as my wrist. I used to milk the cows, separate the calves and feed them before I went to school. If I was late for school, stiff bikkies. So it just came on me that I was a work horse.

Being a cripple wore my father down and he committed suicide. My mother died from a brain tumour four months later. My younger brother was only four and I was eleven. A year later, my elder brother was killed in a truck accident. I don't mind talking about it. I just get sentimental.

My first husband was a timber getter. We'd go out cutting posts, fencing. He and I used to cut the sleepers with a broad axe. That scar, that's the result — thirty-two stitches. I reared my first six kids in the bush, correspondence school. We had to go down to the dam to wash. I'm pretty fit. Had my youngest when I was forty, pretty easy birth — twenty minutes. Suppose if you're crude, it's like shelling peas. I look old in my face I guess, but not in my body — well, not for eight kids.

Then we were up in Darwin. My husband worked hard and he drank hard. He became an alcoholic. I left him because I couldn't hack the pace. I'd work as a barmaid in the daytime, at the laundry at night. Then, about ten, I'd go to the bakery and finish there at four in the morning. Have a couple of hours sleep before I got up to get the kids off to school. I wasn't brainy enough to think about getting the pension. Did it my way and kept the kids, although I finally buggered up and had to put them in a home for a spell. Then I went back to work so I could get them out. They've turned out all right — all married and got kids.

Met Dennis up in Derby. We were going to Perth, but it got so darned cold, I wouldn't go any further. When Coles opened in South Hedland, Dennis said we should try and see what they wanted to do with the greens and vegies they had to throw out. We've got the contract to cart their rubbish away. It feeds the animals.

We've collected a whole stack of animals — kangaroos, emus, camels, donkeys and dogs. People say animals are dumb, but they just can't speak, that's all.

Dennis and I work together all day, so at the end of the day, there's nothing to say to each other. That's why we like hitchhikers. If we're at the pub and there's one on Walkabout Corner waiting for a lift to Broome, we bring him back for a shower, a meal and a bed. We've met people from all over the world. Different natures, different ways of life. You'd never know about it otherwise.

MARIE BROSNAN

Hooley Station, Marie Brosnan's home, is 480 kilometres south-west of Port Hedland. It's almost a two hour drive to get milk and papers at the 'local' store. Dust storms blow the red dirt into every part of the house and the torrential rains can literally sweep through the house. Marie, petite and almost girlish is undefeated by the isolation and the hardships. She loves station life, although much of the rough, brutal work goes against her nature.

I got married at fifteen and had my daughter at sixteen, then my son straight after, then two more daughters. They brought out the pill after I had the last one, but I'm not at all sorry, although the marriage didn't last.

When I met Snow, we just clicked. We decided to leave the city. We didn't have much money so we did roo and horse shooting. I cried when I first saw a horse shot, especially as it wasn't killed outright. I'd sit in the vehicle while Snow did all the hard work. But in the end I saw the poor bugger out there doing it all by himself and I thought it was time I did something.

You've got to take the horses' heads off and I steeled myself to do that. Then I kept at it. Sometimes it would be stinking hot out there, and I'd strip down to my jeans — my bra, shirt, and the rest would be off. In the middle of the bush, hacking up a horse with an axe, blood everywhere.

But I always wear a hat. I'd feel naked without it. And I use moisturiser and makeup. Just because you live out in the bush, you don't let yourself go. We had no washing machine so I'd put the clothes in a plastic bin and tie it in the back of the four wheel drive. We went over such bumpy country that it was almost as good as a machine.

We decided to get Hooley Station. The owners had dumped sheep at the homestead to make it look good. After we arranged the finance and came back up here, the sheep had got into the house and couldn't get out. They were on their last legs and the house was full of manure. It took ages and ages to clean up. There were dead sheep in the well. There was no garden at all, no yards, not even a spanner on the place. We've built it all up from scratch.

At mustering time, I go out mustering every day with Snow. I try and do the dishes and tidy up before we rush off. Jumping over all those rocks gets you pretty fagged, takes it out of you, but there's dinner to cook for up to sixteen men.

I like nice houses. The garden was hard to get going here because there were these monstrous goats and they'd just jump the chicken wire fence I put up and strip everything. We had to shoot them in the end. And the soil's so hard and rocky, it's hard to find plants that'll survive.

I bought paint for the house and painted the outside. I got wallpaper for the bedrooms and the lounge, but the rains ruined the paper. I had carpet, but the house got flooded and it got wrecked. Anything nice — nature rips it down. But I've never let anything get the better of me. I want to make the house look nice and Snow has his heart set on it too. I get put back to square one, but I don't let it get me down. You persevere. Wouldn't be here if you didn't.

JEAN WELSH

Jean and Bidge Welsh have retired to Marble Bar where they now live in a transportable house, just outside town. Yarrie Station, where Jean lived for many years, is now managed by Jean's eldest son. Marble Bar, which has the distinction of being the hottest town in Australia, is a former gold town. There is a resurgence of interest in prospecting there that Bidge and Jean share.

My mother believed we children must have a good education, so we came to Perth but when we went to practising school, we had a different teacher each week. They put us in the country room because they thought we were country bumpkins. I don't know how Mum coped, feeding seven kids. I know we had very little — barley, bread and jam, bread and dripping and figs from the tree in the backyard which we sold to buy more bread.

When I married my first husband, Owen Coppin, it took us a week to come up from Perth to Yarrie. We christened the car Leaping Lena. When we arrived at Yarrie, I saw the old stone house and I remember thinking that it looked all right, with a pretty view and the hills behind. Owen drove me right round the lawn and carried me onto the verandah, which was all slate. They weren't artistic, they were just saving money. I had never seen so many cockroaches in my life. They were everywhere.

There were all the blackfellows to feed. We had to make eight loaves of bread a day. I did have some gins helping me, but I felt that by the time I'd cooked for them as well, I'd rather have done the work myself. I felt I had to carry on the tradition. One old gin, Lucy, resented me, because I was new. She'd been there since Owen was a little boy. Owen told me, 'If you promise them you'll do something, do it.' So one of them wanted me to make her a dress. She was about two axehandles across and I made a band, gathered a skirt and made the top. I thought it was pretty good. She told me it was exactly the same as the ones they made at the next station. She thought I'd come up with a new style and wasn't at all pleased.

It used to take three hours to come sixty miles into town. I'd feel very smart in my spike-heeled shoes, but we'd have to walk down the street and up to the dance hall, by which time all the leather would be off the heels because the road was so rough.

It amazes me that women now go to a doctor as soon as they're pregnant. I used to come into Marble Bar when I was due and stay with the matron. The doctor, always flying or doing something with his aeroplane, was still trying to get the grease off his hands before the baby arrived. I had Sue on VP day during the war. There was a big party on and everyone was so drunk that they'd forgotten to turn the generator on, so there were no lights. The doctor came in the next day and thanked me. We were the only ones in town who didn't have hangovers.

When my husband was killed, I couldn't think of anything except coming back to Yarrie. I felt I belonged. It's a way of life, not an easy way, but you either love it or you hate it. They say if you stay too long, you get the disease. Well, I've got that disease.

I don't know how you'd get on without a sense of humour. You can always look back and laugh. You need more of a one-to-one relationship with your husband. There's not the diversion of someone handsome living round the corner.

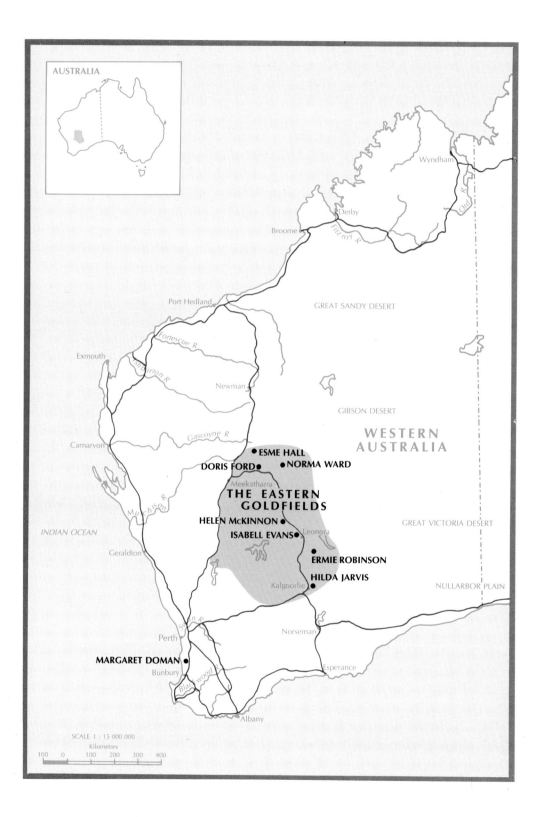

Wyndham

Derby

Broome

Ord R

Fitzroy R

Port Hedland

GREAT SANDY DESERT

Exmouth

Fortescue R

Ashburton R

Newman

GIBSON DESERT

Gascoyne R

Carnarvon

WESTERN
AUSTRALIA

● ESME HALL

DORIS FORD ●   ● NORMA WARD

Murchison R

Meekatharra

THE EASTERN
GOLDFIELDS

INDIAN OCEAN

HELEN McKINNON ●

GREAT VICTORIA DESERT

ISABELL EVANS ●

Leonora

Geraldton

● ERMIE ROBINSON

HILDA JARVIS ●

Kalgoorlie

NULLARBOR PLAIN

Swan R

Perth

Norseman

MARGARET DOMAN ●

Bunbury

Esperance

Blackwood R

Albany

SCALE 1 : 15 000 000

Kilometres

100   0   100   200   300   400

THE EASTERN GOLDFIELDS

The Goldfields of Western Australia are an area where properties are big. The flat, red dirt is sparsely covered with scrub and eucalypt. In the semi-desert climate, the soil is powdery and in the dust storms, there is no escape from it. When it rains, the red dirt turns to a thick, claggy mud that sticks to everything, bogging cars and animals. But the rain also gives immediate life to the land. Plants, lying dormant for months or years, spring into life overnight when the rain comes.

The gold rushes which occurred more than eighty years ago have left their mark on the country. Kalgoorlie is still a prosperous town but elsewhere, throughout the area are ghost towns, abandoned shafts and claims. But there is enough gold to keep the smalltime prospector hopeful that one day he'll make a fortune.

The stations of the Goldfields are so big that there are often no boundary fences and mustering in the far reaches of a property is done with the neighbours. Cattle and sheep are run, but more often cattle because of the prevalence of dingoes. Often, because of the size of properties and the distance between towns, the isolation, for the women in particular, is extreme.

ESME HALL

Ned's Creek Station where Esme Hall lives with her husband, Ken, is 400 000 hectares (a million acres) and hundreds of miles from the nearest big town. The station homestead, with a neat vegetable garden at the back and a small flower garden at the front is incongruously suburban. Esme and Ken have three sons, but for the most part, live by themselves. Their only communication with the outside world is the radio telephone and the mail deliveries.

After I finished boarding school, I went back to Wiluna and worked in the Mines Department. There were about 3000 people in the town then. The only black fellow was the tracker who stayed down at the police station. Now, it's mostly blacks: the only whites are the three policemen and their wives, the people in the garage, the truck driver and the two school teachers.

A girlfriend of mine had a shine for Ken and she kept saying to me that Ken might be coming into town and taking her to the pictures. I didn't know him from a bar of Bedfords, but I met him at a do and we went round together for a bit. I married him in 1952. We came straight out here. In the old homestead, the dust came straight through into the bedroom. I used to cope in those days, because I was young. It's not so easy when you're older.

There weren't any other white women here when I came and we didn't have the pedal radio. It was just Ken and me to start with.

I have three boys. I lost one between Clyde and Walter. I flew down to Perth to have my babies and when they were about three weeks old I flew home and that was that. I taught the boys myself till they were fifteen years old. We'd start at seven in the morning and finish at twelve. If you got behind, you never caught up, so if they wanted to go somewhere with their father they had to catch up on Saturday or Sunday. I'd never had experience teaching. Some people thought I was a bit hard on my boys.

We used not to get any mail at all till we went into town. Now, it comes out every two weeks. We've got the radio phone now, but it hasn't made much difference. I rang my sister when I had to go down to Perth and asked if I could stay with her, but that's more or less the only time we've used it.

Marriage isn't beer and skittles. It's down to tin tacks when the orange blossom of the wedding is gone and forgotten. Now that the children have gone, we've gone full circle, back to just the two of us. Someone asked me the other day how I cope on my own when the men are away. It doesn't bother me. I'm not anti-social, but I could live by myself without any trouble.

DORIS FORD

The Ford house is a traditional Australian country house, homey and comfortable. The family sit round the open fire or share a pot of tea in the kitchen. Even though the eight children are now grown up, the house still tends to be noisy and slightly chaotic, with a strong family atmosphere.

My Dad used to box and decided to teach a few young fellows. John was one of them and I started going out with him. We got engaged and then married in the June — thirty-five years ago next month it'll be. We farmed in Victoria, sheep and wheat. We had eight children and it was hard to expand our farm there. We read about Paroo in *Stock and Land* and we flew up. I always remember getting off that plane in Meekatharra about midnight and thinking what heat there was from the engine. But it wasn't from the engine, it was from the ground.

We bought it and we set off across the Nullarbor: John, myself and the kids in a truck, car and a trailer. I can remember when we finally got here coming through the rabbit-proof gate from Yandill onto the Paroo property — all the beautiful ghost gums and then up to the homestead where there was a whole group of natives. I'd been used to the Swan Hill natives, but these were blacker. There was one old chappy by the name of Tinker who looked quite savage. I never knew how to cook bread when I first came. There was a native woman in the kitchen, Daisy, and she taught me. I've always had to make great quantities of bread.

Sundays, we try to make a bit different here. We eat in what we call the big room, we read the gospel for the day and say grace. I think it makes it just that bit different from other days. I think we have to come back to Christianity to pull the world together.

Our Timothy died from snake bite seven years ago. He was working with his brother-in-law. It was lunch time and he was playing cricket. He rushed into the bush after the ball and rushed out again saying he'd been bitten. He'd had an accident from a horse when he was nine, had his spleen removed, so he didn't have any resistance. He died ten days later. He'd taken out a fair insurance policy, so we decided to build a chapel in memory of him. My brother came over and helped make the mud bricks. The Bishop of the North-West will be coming across to dedicate it for us.

Tim's buried on the property, out near Crystal Well. It's a beautiful, peaceful spot with gum trees, flats and the hills in the distance. You know . . . 'I shall lift mine eyes unto the hills.'

NORMA WARD

*For Norma Ward, looking after injured and sickly animals is just
another part of running a sheep station. She also copes with bringing up
her retarded daughter. On an isolated sheep station, the difficulties of
this job are multiplied many times, but Norma and her husband Rex
overcome them with down-to-earth humour and practicality.*

First met Rex when I was about four, in Wiluna. Not really childhood
sweethearts. To tell you the honest truth, I couldn't stand Rex till I was
about sixteen. Thought he was an arrogant know-all. Couldn't hack him.

Kerri-Lyn seemed quite normal, like any other little baby. Then she
came down with the measles and just went backwards. In Perth they told
us, 'Very poor muscle development, bring her back in three months.'
They couldn't find any minor brain damage, let alone major. They did
find she was deaf. I'd take her down every three months. Cost $500 and
the doctors would say, 'She'll be walking in six months. You're doing a

good job.' Six months would pass, then another, then a year and she was no closer to walking than I was to flying to the moon. On one visit, I had seven appointments. The sociologist told me she was worried — she thought our social life mightn't be spot on because of our retarded child.

The doctor told me she'd be walking in six months, the physio said the same. I finally told them to stop beating round the bush. They told me they'd just been trying to keep my morale up and she wouldn't walk till she was ten. Then they couldn't understand why I wasn't upset. They'd had mothers who'd just walked out on their kids. I told them that these kids don't ask to be born. It's not our fault nor their fault. You have to make the best of it.

Someone put me onto the Doman Delacato program. I work a daily four-hour program with Kerri-Lyn. She does an hour of horse riding. I get on behind her and when we trot, I hang onto her plaits. It was hard when Christopher started school, doing it with his and her program. When we went out on the horse, I'd have to toss him on behind with a reading book or a maths book. When I had to go out to help Rex fix a mill or something, we'd take Christopher's table and Kerri-Lyn's pusher. Now he stays at Granite Peak and does his school with his cousin, which is marvellous for him.

Rex and I love arguing. It's part of him and it's part of me, but never have one of us said 'It's your fault Kerri-Lyn is like that.' I'm sure Rex hates taking me out, because I usually see a poor sheep that's a bit decrepit and pounce on it. He says, 'It needs knocking, you're not taking it home.' It's on for young and old and we have a real domestic out there in the scrub.

Had a little lamb that'd had its eyes pecked out by crows. We patched him up and called him Boppo. When we slept out on the lawn, he'd sleep under the bed, like a dog. One night, lying there, he started groaning. I thought he'd poisoned himself, so I rubbed his belly for an hour till he went to sleep. The next night he started again and Rex thought he must be eating something to poison himself. I rubbed again and the third night it started again. I decided to take a good look and shone the torch down. He was just chewing his cud. Boppo got a boot in the backside for his trouble.

HELEN McKINNON

Pinnacles Station is one of the oldest, wealthiest and best known sheep stations of the area. It is an old family station, with a feeling of solidity. The lovely old homestead with its garden, cricket pitch, pool and guest-house reflects the lifestyle that has been established and refined over two generations.

Because of the isolation out here and the demands put on women to create a happy home, a career must come second. I used to be an air hostess. It was a lot of fun because Western Australia was really opening up — places like Tom Price and Port Hedland. I was single and I didn't have the responsibilities I have now.

Sometimes here, it's like running an institution. We employ a full-time gardener, several jackaroos, a governess and a girl to help run the house. When we're mustering or shearing, you make the lunches and have to remember who wants thick or thin bread and how thick they like their Vegemite.

It's fabulous having people around and there's a terrific spirit here. We have a lot of fun. We don't worry about nine to five, you knock off when the work's done. After work in summer, they'll go out and play cricket with my husband. Or they'll sit out on the back lawn and have a beer. Sometimes on Sundays, the staff play tennis and we occasionally have

people out from the local mining town for a challenge match. They might stay for a barbecue or a swim.

One of the biggest things out here is the education of your children. I taught my three for two years, then I felt I was getting stale. I thought it was time to get a governess who could offer them music and art.

It's great having a good season and being able to afford staff. Seasonal conditions really dictate how easy things will be. We've got the staff now, because of the good rains, but you can sometimes have too much. In 1975 we had two years' rainfall in four days. We were very composed about it. We'd just killed a beast and were sitting down to a piece of roast beef. The water just flowed across the floor. It was ten inches deep in the house for two nights and we all slept on the back of a truck. We had a sick Aboriginal child here and eventually the civil defence landed and took us to the local town.

It took six months to clean the house and we lost three thousand ewes and the young sheep just drowned. It happened just after the cyclone in Darwin and a Natural Disasters Committee had been set up. Pastoralists can't afford to insure fencing or stock for flood loss. So we applied to the Natural Disasters Committee but only got $400 for some long ball dresses of mine that were ruined. Losing so much was very depressing. It takes a long time to build it up again.

SABELL EVANS

The Oasis Vegetable Farm is about twenty kilometres out of the town of Leonora. It is a beautifully kept plot of ten hectares (twenty-four acres). It is an old gold claim and Isabell tends it lovingly, producing an extraordinary array of fresh vegetables. Sometimes, she takes off to see relatives or go prospecting, but never for too long.

I wouldn't know when I was born. My Dad might know about it. Out of the three in my family, only me and my brother now. He's in Kalgoorlie and his wife and family live in Leonora. I lost my sister. When my mother was alive, we live in Leonora, a lot bigger then. But she went to the mission. I lost my mother there. She die there. I got one boy — he's in Laverton somewhere now, out at the mission.

I been all my life on the stations. You know, go station to station. Don't sit around, do a job — housework, cooking sometimes, horse riding, muster the sheep and cattle.

Now Jack and me been here four years. I known Jack all my blinking life, no, about ten years. There's big ocean water under the earth. That windmill you pass, that's where we get the pipeline to run to pump the water into the garden. You feel you want to do things, you do it. Make you feel funny when you don't do anything. Lots of people come and want fresh vegies.

We go out for the gold, prospecting. Sometimes, we get up at sunrise, light the fire. We got all we need out there. It doesn't matter where you go. We had fair bit of luck. Alluvial gold, that's hard to get now.

I go out and get rabbit, kangaroos, goannas when we feel like it. Do some carving too, with the mulga needle bush. That prickly bush — you go out, find a nice bendy one and just chop that, cut it in two and trim it and make it up nice and fine, burn the patterns on it. Lovely stockwhip handle. It just come like nature to me. We see how to do all them things.

ERMIE ROBINSON

Yerilla Station is a big family property, of 100 000 hectares (250 000 acres). Ermie and her husband, Bruce, run the property as a partnership, sharing the outdoor and indoor work. Both have interests besides the land — in politics and the arts — and they set aside time to enjoy and develop these together.

I went to university in Perth in 1970, which was a very interesting time — the time of the Vietnam moratorium. Being in the politics department, which was very left wing, I became fairly involved. Now, I'm politically to the right. I think that's because I went out into the world and discovered you don't get something for nothing. But I'm still a member of the Women's Electoral Lobby and I care about abortion law reform and those social issues.

I would have never dreamt of just getting married and coming up here. I think you have to find out whether you can stand each other's company and the environment first. It's more important to be good friends and to be able to have a conversation at night about things other than the station. Bruce enjoys the ballet and opera whereas a lot of fellows don't. When we go to Perth, I've got someone to share it with. It makes a difference to our relationship.

The rural scene and the attitude to women annoys me. Women here in the bush are underrated, except in the kitchen. If there wasn't a need for creature comforts, a lot of men would be perfectly happy not to have women in the bush.

I couldn't stand to be home all the time. The best part for me is to be out on a motorbike mustering, but then lots of women couldn't stand that, or working with sheep — and why should they? I've been involved in the Pastoralists and Graziers Association. You can get yourself noticed at a conference if you're one of the few women there. But one thing that really annoys me is that at the sheep and wool sections of the conference, they'll have a fashion parade and boat trip for the women while the men talk business. It's a subtle put down: 'you wouldn't really be interested'. Men tend to discount what you say, as a 'woman's point of view' as if that is somehow different. It's as if they believe the rural industry depends on whether you can get a column out of a well.

When I came up here, we had two summers of bushfires. I really got to know the neighbours. It was a time of crisis and all the barriers were down. It revived that community spirit that had gone in the drought.

There's great freedom up here — people not wheeling prams into you in the streets, not looking at you to see if you're properly dressed, whether you're going broke or getting fat. I see friends in Perth and my life experiences in the last ten years have been so totally different that we have only the past in common. It's not enough to keep a friendship going. Bruce is my mate now — my best friend and companion.

HILDA JARVIS

Hilda Jarvis lives in a small cottage, crammed with memories of the past. It is in the old town of Bulong, a former gold prospecting town, that, today, is virtually a ghost town. She used to live at Hampton Hill Station, which was taken up by her father and is now run by a nephew.

In Bulong, Dad had a general store, a gold buyer's licence and a licence to sell so many bottles of beer. He was a JP and mayor of the town twice. Father would help some of the miners with groceries, said he couldn't see them starve, so when they left, father was often left a house — actually just a corrugated iron shack.

When I was four, he bought Hampton Hill Station. Mum used to milk eighteen cows of a morning, separate the milk and make butter to sell. Old Madame Vauthier was a French woman who came to help mother with the ironing. She wasn't 'madame' really, it was just a courtesy. She was a nice old thing really, but you know what French women are like. She had a chappy, Jack Frost was his name. She never married him but she always had her joker. No one thought anything of it. I'd ask mother and mother would say. 'Oh Hilda, she's French!'

We used goats for milk and meat. Dad would sell goat meat in town for sixpence a pound. Now, goats are part of my life. Some fellows come out and shoot them, so I keep my favourites tied up. My son George lives with me, but he's away prospecting quite a bit. You'd have seen that shaft on the side of the road, he sunk that one, 150 feet, all on his own. One night there were two cars and four young blokes came out, two in the morning. They told me they were just out for a spin and asked if I had any gins out here. I told them I don't harbour that sort and to get.

I hate drink, never touch it, but I always keep a bottle of brandy just in case someone needs it. Often, I'll give a little bit to a kid that needs to be revived. Had one last week. Couldn't save it. It died that night. Its poor mother kept coming up to me the next morning. She knew I took it. So I said to George that I'd take it down to the yards so she could see it. The nanny saw it and lay down next to it for two hours. She'd get up now and then, bleating. It was heartbreaking really, but she hasn't asked me since.

ARGARET DOMAN

Margaret Doman is well known in Western Australia for her interest in horses and her incredibly wide knowledge of them. She is a real bushwoman, who works extremely hard and was totally involved in the station life.

As a girl, I lived a life of horses, hunters and shows. I won the reserve champion hack at Melbourne show in 1934. In 1939, when war broke out, Father bought properties over here in Western Australia. He increased his holdings. He had a natural gift of picking something good. I came over in 1942 by train across the Nullarbor. By 1946, he'd bought properties up near Wiluna. The country there is marginal, but a good breeding area. We breed up there and bring stock down to fatten.

I was always my father's girl. I was very friendly with one young chap, but it didn't work out and I never really cast my eye around. When my father died we had seven stations up north and over 20 000 acres of farm land, a sheep station in South Australia and one in New South Wales. I looked after the lot because my two sisters are married and my brother, Fred, is a doctor.

Oakford is my favourite property. Dad bought it for me in 1943 and I lived there for twenty-five years. I had a housekeeper and six men. I had to travel up north to see the cattle off on the Canning Stock Route, make sure stores were there and the transceiver sets were working. Up there, you simply had to ride a horse. There were no motor cars, just an old truck for stores. We'd even use camels and pack horses to muster the stock.

I like being alone, being able to have breakfast in my dressing gown. I find I'm doing it more nowadays.

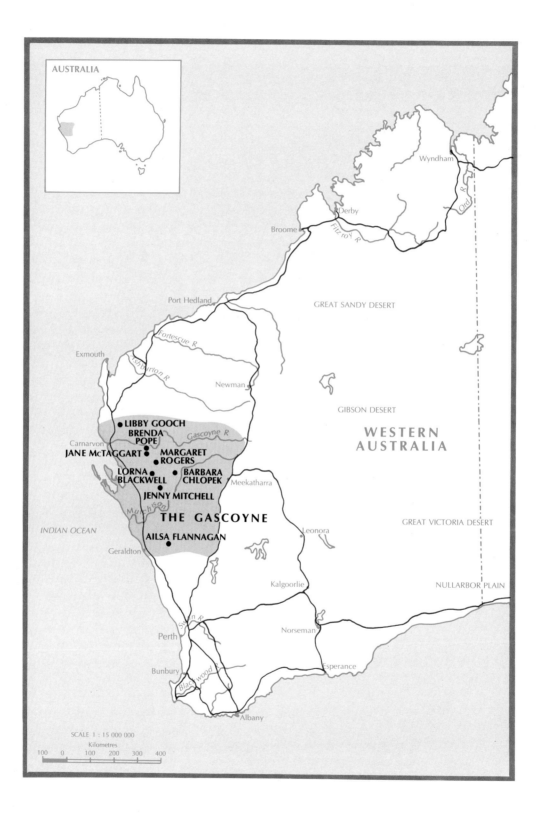

AUSTRALIA

Wyndham

Derby

Broome

Port Hedland

Fortescue R.

Exmouth

Ashburton R.

GREAT SANDY DESERT

Newman

GIBSON DESERT

● LIBBY GOOCH

BRENDA
POPE

Gascoyne R.

Carnarvon

JANE McTAGGART ●

● MARGARET
ROGERS

WESTERN
AUSTRALIA

LORNA
BLACKWELL ●

● BARBARA
CHLOPEK

Meekatharra

JENNY MITCHELL ●

Murchison R.

THE GASCOYNE

INDIAN OCEAN

● AILSA FLANNAGAN

GREAT VICTORIA DESERT

Leonora

Geraldton

Kalgoorlie

NULLARBOR PLAIN

Norseman

Swan R.

Perth

Esperance

Bunbury

Blackwood R.

Albany

Fitzroy R.

Ord R.

SCALE 1 : 15 000 000

Kilometres

100   0   100   200   300   400

THE WHEAT BELT TO THE GASCOYNE

When the wheat is being sown, there are great bare expanses of soil. Only a few scrubby trees have been left for shade. The country undulates slightly, but the overall impression is one of heat and dust. There are fewer big stations here, but it's possible to make a reasonable living on a smaller holding.

North of the wheat belt, in the Murchison and Gascoyne regions, there are more of the sprawling old homesteads, families who've been established for generations. The countryside varies from thickly timbered areas of native scrub and eucalyptus to sandhills and stony plains. The average rainfall is less than 400 mm a year. After the rain, there are masses of everlasting yellow daisies everywhere. At the town of Gascoyne Junction, there's the pub and the bowser. The nearest town, Carnarvon, is 320 kilometres away. The flat, sandy sheep country, dotted with eucalypts and river gums is dominated by the spectacular Kennedy Ranges.

AILSA FLANNAGAN

The work of a station, of caring for a family and a homestead, eat into time relentlessly. Only Ailsa Flannagan's energy, vitality and determination make it possible for her to continue her career as a painter.

I was brought up on Challymanda and by the strangest chance I ended up here again. It came up for sale and my husband, Alf, decided to buy it. I'd been a professional artist before I married. I married quite late, at thirty-six and I decided that my painting wouldn't interfere with my marriage, or my children if I had any. But now, the children are away at boarding school and Mum's come down to help me so I can get an exhibition together. I paint under my maiden name, Ailsa Small. Alf's marvellous about it, but he says I should get a wider brush so I'll finish faster.

As a child, I just wanted to work on my art. At the end of school, I was offered a scholarship to go overseas, but I didn't take it up. I wanted to continue doing representational paintings. I just wasn't interested in the modern stuff they were doing overseas. My father had taught me and he'd been taught by his uncle, a Royal Academy artist. My parents were marvellous, supporting and encouraging me in every way.

Over the centuries, women have been expected to paint dainty little floral arrangements in watercolours and it was expected that the men would paint the more dramatic things — things that supposedly wouldn't suit a woman's personality. It's only the last few years that women have been taken seriously as artists.

I enjoy this life immensely. I'm really an outback person. My parents and I had always planned to come back up north when my father retired. When he died, Mum and I decided to go ahead anyway. We bought a stationwagon and camping gear. Our friends were absolutely horrified, but we were used to the outback and quite capable of changing tyres or fixing up little things — probably better than most men. We camped out in the bush. We were bush people, so we weren't intimidated by the open spaces.

I met Alf on the trip and we sort of grew on each other and enjoyed each other's company. We farm about 9000 acres in all — wheat and sheep. Cropping's constant work. We're seeding now and after that we'll have to spray for weeds, then harvest. We're always reliant on the weather. Alf's a farmer so he just copes and hopes. Up north it's tough for the men and just hard, plain hard, for the women.

JENNY MITCHELL

Jenny Mitchell is one of the new generation of countrywomen, concerned with all aspects of rural life. In times of hardship Jenny has to run Muggon station alone, a job that's both physically and emotionally demanding. When seasons are good, she continues her work on the station but also has time for other interests. She has energetically created a garden around the homestead and is deeply involved in local shire and farm politics and the Country Women's Association.

When Bill and I were first married and came up to Muggon we had a

windmill man, a mechanic, two blackfellows and a jackaroo. The place was very run down, though. One day the mail truck came out and its battery went flat. We had to start a bike with another bike and then it was like a chariot pull to get the Holden going to pull the Toyota four-wheel drive to get that going to pull the old truck, which could pull the mail truck.

The drought hit us and, by 1979, we couldn't afford any help. It was just Bill and I. We had five years' drought. It's an insidious thing. You see the sheep getting poorer and poorer and then they start to die. The men in the district gradually become more depressed, the parties less jovial. The one way we kept our heads above water was with the feral goats. You could get $20 for a good billy goat when sheep were selling for three or four dollars. There was also a bounty for goat ears — a dollar for a set of ears. When the dams dried up, the goats used to go into them and get bogged in the mud. Bill was out doing contract mustering, away for weeks at a time, so there was just the jillaroo and me here. When we did the mill runs we'd go into the dams and cut off the goats' ears. It was pretty gruesome with them stuck there dying and us jumping around cutting off their ears, poor things. We'd also scrape the wool off the dead sheep. We had to — it was money.

Murchison shire is very close knit, with only twenty-seven rate payers, but no town, which means meetings are always held at a station. We all have the same interests — stations, horses, windmills and sheep. Bill has been president of the shire for a year so he's still away a lot. I'm not involved in the running of the shire, but I'm secretary of the Liberal Party here, president of the CWA and delegate for the Pastoralists and Graziers. I'm the token woman.

When Bill goes away. I take over the reins here. I enjoy it, but things always seem to go wrong. During the drought, we had a sudden flood of rain. There wasn't a single room in the house that didn't leak except the office, so I had my bed tucked in there. I couldn't work anywhere else because of the water swirling round the house. I didn't get scared. We've grown used to Muggon being off the beaten track, no one ever comes up here. But I haven't ever been too lonely because there's always something to do. I'm always busy, busy, busy.

BARBARA CHLOPEK

Country people are often branded as conservative and dismissive of people who are different. Barbara Chlopek and her husband Peter don't fit the traditional country image, but they are admired for their hard work and strength of purpose.

I met Peter when I was about seventeen. We decided to leave Melbourne and kept driving — all the way to Perth. We were broke so we answered an ad in the paper and ended up on a station the following week. We didn't know what to do when we went for an interview. We didn't say we weren't married. They assumed we were. Eventually we got married last year.

On stations in the old days, managers could get involved and get shares in the property. They could buy the place over the years. Today, there isn't the opportunity to get further than being a manager. We want to get some money together so one day we can have a property of our own. A shooting licence came up so Peter decided to get it. The licence is only

$25, but then we had to set up the Toyota with loading gear, freezer containers and all that stuff.

Things weren't too good at first with the drought and then they brought out a movie against the kangaroo shooting. It's complete bullshit. Shooters do it as a livelihooc — they're not going to muck round playing skinning a live joey or seeing how long they can drag out the death. They shoot to kill. It's not as if Peter likes killing, but it's a necessity. The roos only survive because there have been windmills put in to provide water. There was no water here before. It's culling, not indiscriminate slaughter. Anyway, the government felt they had to do something, so they've kept the quotas down to last year's level. It's unrealistic because last year was a drought year. So Peter has to do contract work for the shire putting in grids and mustering for shearing. It's lucky that he's a jack of all trades.

I miss him when he's away, but it's no use sooking, ranting and raving. I used to go with him before I had the baby. I've only had six months of motherhood, but it's pretty hard in the heat. When we moved here to Byro Station, I decided if I didn't make an effort to go out and join a few activities, I'd just be sitting at home talking to myself. My mother and my mother-in-law are very involved in the CWA in Victoria and I'd always thought 'Ugh, no way!' But I joined and it's good.

Originally, we gave ourselves five years, but I can see it being a lot longer now. A couple of days ago, Peter was coming back from the shire and hit a roo — bit ironic for a roo shooter. He rolled the Land Rover and it's badly mashed up. We weren't insured. Couldn't afford it. We're back to square one.

JANE McTAGGART

Bidgemia Station is an old, established station owned by the McTaggart family company. Its 400 000 hectares are well maintained and although there are many people employed there, Jane McTaggart has a full-time job keeping things running smoothly and looking after her two children.

I get lonely sometimes for my old friends or my parents, but we are really very fortunate because there are a lot of people here on the station and lots of people call in. Sometimes, there's not quite enough privacy. We're feeding eight people at the moment — that's normal for this time of year. I used to do most of the cooking myself, but I couldn't manage it with the children, so now I have a cook and a yardman.

I love the shearing here. We usually shear in May, but we're a bit late this year because of the rain and the four-year drought before that. We're very fortunate because we're a family company and we get a wage.

The mail truck comes out every Wednesday from Carnarvon. We put our orders in on Mondays and everything we need comes out — fuel, parts and stores. In summer when you get the tropical, cyclonic rain, we stock up with bulk fuel and we have a special store for non-perishable items. But fuel's the big thing — if you run out of that, you're buggered.

I have at least two parties a year where I have over a hundred people. I cater easily because we have big kitchens and freezers, but I ask people to bring things because you can't afford to be throwing big parties like that. It's usually for something like the Liberal Party or for someone well known who's leaving the district. The Gascoyne Junction races are the major annual event for us. Lachie does a lot of the organising and we have a lot of people staying here for the weekend. They come on Friday

evening and camp till Monday. Friday night is a big dance and get
together for the station people. Saturday's race day, with tourists and
people from Carnarvon. Monday's never good because that's the clean up
day with a lot of hangovers.

We had a native yardman, Jack, a terrific old bloke. He died two years
ago on Christmas Day, so that Christmas was a real letdown for us. He'd
gone out the night before on the booze with two other black fellows. Old
Jack had a stroke. They brought him in very early. They were very upset
about it. They get like that with death — think the feather foots are after
them. He was only just alive, five breaths a minute. We called the flying
doctor and sent him off. But the two who brought him in must have had
a fight, because round about three o'clock a gin appeared with a gash
right down the back of her head. I looked after the wound, and I'd just
about had it, but she was quite cheerful. I asked her how it happened and
she told me, 'That Brian, he should work for Beaurepaires the way he
handles that tyre lever.'

Romance of life here? Basically, it's just hard yakka. It might have been different when the place was in full swing with natives and lots of staff. They had gins sweeping the floors and the verandahs. Now, it's different. We live amongst a whole heap of chauvinists. It's definitely a man's world out here. Aren't they lucky we fit in?

BRENDA POPE

The outback abounds with jokes about shearer's cooks — mainly the quantity of their alcohol intake and the quality of the food they produce. But being a shearer's cook boils down to extraordinarily hard work for the eight or nine months of the shearing season. Brenda Pope works with a contractor around the Gascoyne area, moving with the team from station to station. The hours are long and the work is physically hard.

I came from England in 1968. The kids were only ten, six and two. I had to leave them at Fairbridge Farm School and couldn't get them back till I settled on a farm in Geraldton two years later. Geraldton was an accident. I was in Perth and I had enough money for a train either to Bunbury or Geraldton. I wanted to go to Bunbury, but I went to the wrong desk. He told me the platform and I just arrived in Geraldton at six next morning. I was tired, cold and hungry. I found the old Great Northern Guest House. The guy there was really nice — he gave me a job straight away helping in the laundry.

Then I got a job cooking on the property, then worked in the cray factory and bars but eventually got a little place for me and the kids just out of Geraldton. God, did we have fun there! It was an old tomato grower's place, just twelve dollars a week, a big tin shed divided up. We had a shower recess but no shower, so me and the kids went up to the tip and stole a bath tub, put it in the shower recess, gave it a good clean and had a bath. We found some rusty old rabbit traps and used to trap rabbits to eat or to sell to the butcher. I used to walk into the butcher's so I got to know all the people and made a living picking peas and doing the vegie gardens and stuff. It was pretty hard, but everything we had, we'd got ourselves. Even the kids would work when they came home from school. It was hard at times. The kids kept me going. There were nights when I cried myself to sleep, but the kids didn't see that.

I got the sack from my first shearing team. They reckon I didn't make enough different meals. But they were animals — there wasn't even a trough in the kitchen to wash the dishes. The guy told me to finish up that night. I took off my apron and told him I was finished right there and then. I've been in different teams since. In general, shearers are a pretty good mob. If they get heavy, I'm quite capable of telling them off. You get to know how to handle them. Some of the girls have trouble with guys going down to their rooms. I think women's lib is a lot of rot. Women are women and they'll always be treated that way. It's up to the individual to decide how she wants to be treated.

In the mornings, I like to get up at five. Having the wood stove, it takes longer. I make lamb's fry, eggs, maybe sausages, toast. I do the eggs as they walk in. The shearers pay for the mess and my wages, so I try to make it like home. Getting the toast right can be a bit of a problem on a fuel stove.

When we move, I have to pack all the stuff and the boys help me carry the boxes out. I find I have to play Mum. Sometimes there are problems, serious ones. You've got to be everything in this job — tactician, politician, mother, nurse, the lot.

ARGARET ROGERS

Margaret and her husband, Ron, started with nothing. Like many outback couples, they work as a team. They bought Carey Downs Station, built a new homestead and are expanding further. Margaret is wife, mother, cook, station hand and financier.

When I married Ron in 1970, we went back east where he was shearing. I was only just tolerated, because women round the shearing sheds in those days weren't the thing at all. Ron told me to stay away from the shed. They didn't like the women because they couldn't swear when they were around. When Ron wrote to one of the contractors to ask if he could bring me along, the contractor wrote back that, it was 'neither advisable nor possible, in that order'. Ron decided to take me anyway and eventually they got used to it. The contractor even got quite proud of it and would boast he had the first caravan and the first baby on the team. But we had to keep away from the camp, because neither of the babies slept and if there's one thing shearers need, it's their sleep.

The worst part with the children was having to pack up every three weeks so when we arrived here in 1975, I thought it was marvellous, because we didn't have to move on. That was, until it started to rain and everything leaked, the wind blew and every room filled with dust and debris and the walls started to fall down and the ceilings dropped. But I suppose it's better than a lot of people have.

We always went out together to do things. Ron needed rocks because he was building a tank. I remember sitting on the hillside breastfeeding the baby. As time went on, the kids were useful too and sometimes they couldn't sit down and do their school work because they had to help. If we were going for the whole day, we'd pack lunch, a table and the school work, but sometimes they'd work on their knees or in the Land Rover. They'd come to me for help and I'd wipe the cement off my hands and try to work with them. I'd put notes into the teacher that the maths is a bit messy because we'd been out bush or doing the shearing.

I don't think the children really suffered. I can see that from the report my eldest got from high school. I've suffered because of the guilt feelings they could have done better at primary level. My dream is to take the kids to the zoo. When I was a kid, I remember going to the museum, the zoo and riding on a train. They're simple things, but I know my kids would love the zoo.

These days, you can't afford to go and visit someone solely for social contact. There has to be a good business excuse. I miss having a really close friend, someone you could more or less bare your heart to.

LORNA BLACKWELL

The isolation of Callytharra Station sometimes makes Lorna Blackwell cautious with strangers. But Lorna has been waiting a long time to tell her life story. She and George live in complete harmony with their environment. They have their goats, they feed cockatoos and have horses and cattle. It's hard and it's poor, but satisfying.

I was nine and we were living in a tent at a place called Pithara. My mother gave birth to my brother in the tent. Father said to me, 'Mum's sick. Find a horse and ride over to the next farm.' That was seven miles away. It was really dark and I had trouble finding the horse. I came back and I saw Mum lying on the bed. She was blue and I knew she was dead.

I never forgave my father for that. He'd been cruel to her even before the baby was born. She used to have to help sink her own wells and things like that.

Men are hard. Through my life, I've been in love with quite a few men. I married once and I've been living with George for twenty-eight years now. A man is like a bull — you never know when he's going to turn and kick you in the arse.

I worked around farms and in 1935 I married Ted Blackwell who was working on the same farm. He was English and the English are terrible hard on their women. I borrowed two bags of flour off my stepmother, and bakehouse tins and we went down to Calingiri. There was an old bakehouse down there and we re-opened it and started working there, but we couldn't make a living. So we went to Coorow and we were there for thirteen years, right through the war. Then we went down to Mount Helena and got a little farm, but we couldn't make a living, so we went back to Perth. Ted got leukemia and only lasted a little while. He died in 1956.

I'd met George when we were at Coorow. His mother was a half caste and she'd come to chop wood for me. George was always a stockman, since he was eighteen. My first husband used to drink and I liked

George because he didn't drink or smoke. So I wrote to him after Ted died and he came straight down. We got matey and I came back up here to Callytharra Springs. There was only the old spinifex shed up then. We put some iron on it and lived there for a couple of years. George had about eighty head of cattle and seven horses. When I first came here, I used to go everywhere with him. We built it up and up and up.

Once we went up the river and got into trouble. But we weren't stealing cattle, only picking up cleanskins and our own cattle. Our neighbours went and got the police, reckoned we were pinching theirs. Well, we did have three of theirs and there's a law you don't put them in yards, so I went back and scattered them. They could never pin anything on us, so we ended up in the clear.

Marriage is very important to me. But with George, his wife ran away with another man. His intention was to get a divorce and to marry me, but he changed his mind. Thought he'd like children. I told him that I couldn't have children and suggested we adopt them. 'I don't want anyone else's bastards,' he told me, which was a bit of a kick in the pants for me.

We've survived. We could live off the bush and goats. We don't spend on clothes or things. The only money we owe on the station now is for fuel. We're the only ones up round here that don't have a bank loan. We live humble.

LIBBY GOOCH

Isolation is a fact of life in the bush. Because they don't have a normal social life, most women have very strong partnerships with their men. When Libby Gooch's husband died in a mustering accident, Libby not only lost her partner, but also had to take over his role on the station.

I was left with three young children. They had to go away to school. My husband left his shares to the children and I was the employed manager. I went in to see the state manager at Elders who told me the best thing to do was to get back to the station and get the shearing through. I thought him cold, cruel and callous but I did it.

The first few years were disappointing. I'd ask the men why the sheep were looking awful, why this, why that. They wouldn't answer. It was very embarrassing. They obviously didn't know and I wasn't getting anywhere. I had one full blood native with me and I learnt so much from him. He'd stop in the bush: 'Come with me, Missus, I show you

something.' When we were out mustering, he'd say, 'Just push them over the hill Missus, let them go down the gully, let them drift. We just stay, let them wander down on their own.' On my own, I would have stayed behind, pushing. He taught me how to track, staying on the outside of the tracks, never on the inside. Then you know they're in the middle somewhere.

I used to camp out a lot, only with this one native because I knew I was protected by him. I could never thank him enough for all he did. It's sad — those old blokes were so good, but I wouldn't go out the back gate at night with these young half castes.

When we're mustering, we're gone by four in the morning, muster all day and I've got to get back here to cook for the native staff. I do everybody's washing and ironing, cut all the lunches, make cakes and biscuits. It's nothing for me to go to bed after two in the morning.

You come in and you're tired and filthy and you think, 'Blow it all'. But I always take my boots off, have a shower, change and cream my face and hands. I even put perfume on. It'd be so easy just to let yourself go, let your whole morale slide.

I don't think there'd be many men left up here without the women. Women work equally as hard as men do, harder, because the men have only the outside work to do. But I believe in a man being head of the household.

I'd like to hand over and get back to being the mother, housewife, the woman here. I'm too young to retire but I want a break. I'm sick of climbing up windmills, lifting columns, going down wells. I'm past that age and stage. I did it when I was younger and it was fun. When my son's ready to take over, I'll move to Perth and stay there. Maybe he'll need me back here to bake him a cake or something.

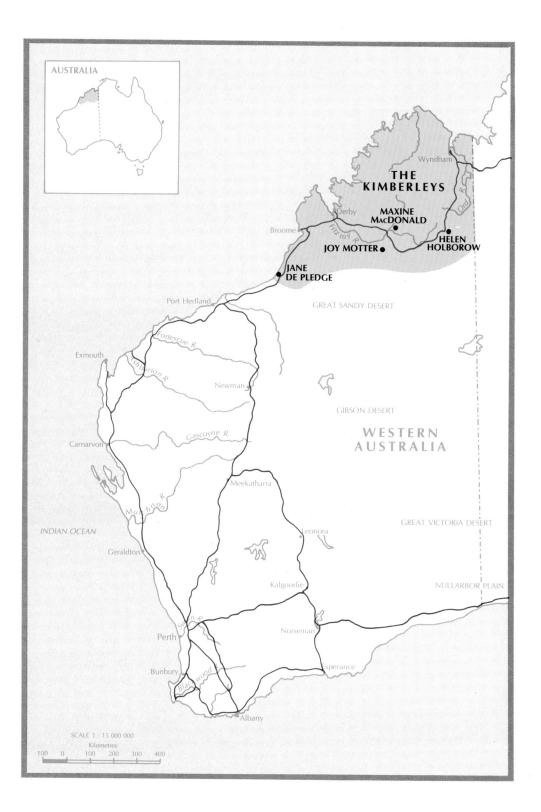

AUSTRALIA

THE KIMBERLEYS

Wyndham

MAXINE MacDONALD

Derby

Broome

HELEN HOLBOROW

JOY MOTTER

JANE DE PLEDGE

Port Hedland

GREAT SANDY DESERT

Fortescue R.

Exmouth

Ashburton R.

Newman

GIBSON DESERT

Gascoyne R.

Carnarvon

WESTERN AUSTRALIA

Meekatharra

Murchison R.

GREAT VICTORIA DESERT

INDIAN OCEAN

Leonora

Geraldton

Kalgoorlie

NULLARBOR PLAIN

Perth

Swan R.

Norseman

Bunbury

Esperance

Blackwood R.

Albany

SCALE 1 : 15 000 000
Kilometres
100   0   100   200   300   400

WOMEN OF THE KIMBERLEYS

The Kimberley Region is spectacular country, with its craggy ridges and deep gorges. It is real cattle country. In the dry, feed is sparse but when the rains come, the rich soil responds and grass grows almost overnight, thick and lush. There are the exotic baobab trees, with their large, swollen trunks. Frequently there are mirages on the hot, shimmering plains. The properties are big and the towns few and far between. For women, the isolation is often extreme and they must find the resources to create their own world.

M AXINE MacDONALD

Fossil Downs is set in amongst the ranges. Both the house and the setting have almost a film set quality — the harsh beauty of the landscape, the extravagant stone staircase and black and white tiled foyer of the house. It is a setting that suits Maxine MacDonald.

When I left school, I did some modelling and I worked for Warner Brothers Motion Pictures. I met my husband Bill, on one of the old ships that went between Sydney and Fremantle.

Bill's family came up to this country from New South Wales. Why they chose to come that distance from Goulburn, where they had several properties, I will never know, although they had received a report from the explorer, Forrest, describing the leases as being black soil plains with the rivers running all year round. I've been here forty-six years and I've only seen that happen twice.

The family's initial droving trip was one of the longest in the world —

it took them four years to get here. They struck drought in Queensland, lost stock, had to go back and start again. They were right behind the Duracks. On one occasion, Willy MacDonald walked into Durack's camp and one of the Duracks nearly shot him, thinking he was a blackfellow.

I arrived in 1938. On New Year's Day, 1939, we pegged out the foundations of this house. The war interfered with the building, but the roof was on, so they turned it into military headquarters. When the first bombs fell on Broome, Derby and Wyndham, the builders decided Perth was a much nicer place and they vacated.

A lot of women north of the twenty-sixth parallel were evacuated down south, but I was allowed to stay because I did all the coding and decoding over the radio. General Gordon Bennett came up here in a Hudson Bomber. 'This will be a very nice home if it escapes the Japanese, Mrs MacDonald.' He was firmly convinced the Japanese would invade.

All the bricks for the house were made here in the river bed. We had 10 000 in the river at one time. We knew all the air force chaps who flew over and one day we got a message that the Margaret River was running a banker much higher up. Because it's such a long river, it can run even when we've had no rain whatsoever. So we rushed down and worked right through the night to get the last brick out at seven thirty the next morning. Then we went looking for the beastly river and found it five miles up.

Once, I went six months without seeing another white woman. My mother sent me a new frock and I got all dressed up like a bunch of cocky's feathers to go to Fitzroy Crossing. We got to the river and it was running, but not very deep. My husband decided to carry me across to save me undoing my stockings. In the middle, he fell in a hole and dropped me. My beautiful new frock began to shrink immediately. So I didn't arrive at Fitzroy looking quite as glamorous as I'd expected.

The natives here had never seen a fair-haired woman before. If I cut my hair, they'd fight to grab the pieces. We had no electricity, not even kero fridges. We had a Coolgardie safe, made out of timber and hessian. In the middle of winter, if you were lucky and the wind was blowing in the right direction, you might set a jelly. But it didn't matter. I was young, newly wed and very much in love.

JOY MOTTER

People in the outback never take medical services for granted. Doctors and nurses are some of the most important people in a district. Even though it is some years since Joy Motter nursed at Fitzroy Crossing, she is still thought of as a nurse. Today, she and her husband Jim manage Cherrabun Station, where she continues to make use of her nursing skills.

My parents were staunch Presbyterians so I was brought up on a steady diet of John Flynn. He was the minister who invented the pedal radio and established the Flying Doctor Service. The outback always appealed to me and in 1968 I was posted to Fitzroy Crossing.

The majority of the patients were Aboriginals. At that stage, there were about 300 Aboriginals in the town itself, the rest were out on stations. Christmas Creek alone had 300 and Go-Go had two hundred and fifty. It

wasn't till 1971 when the Pastoral Award came in and they all had to be paid basic wages, that they came into town. The pastoralists couldn't afford to pay them.

It used to be mainly chest infections, diarrhoea, cuts and the normal things everyone suffers from. After they got their drinking rights, you'd be patching up broken bones, stitching wounds from fights and arguments — injury based nursing. Today, there's a lot more venereal disease too. There's more mining camps, road camps and tourists — all sorts wandering through. It adds to the breakdown of Aboriginal culture.

The itinerant nursing service was oriented towards teaching Aboriginals preventative medicine — immunisation and trying to build up their diets because they weren't eating their bush tucker any more.

Night flights used to be pretty dangerous. You had to argue with the chap in charge on the phone — whether it was worth his life or the patient's life. You really had to convince him. Once, we had a child who was dying. The plane was due in at midnight and there wasn't any lighting, so we had to organise kero flares on the strip. We were waiting, watching the plane's lights coming closer and closer. One of the sisters held the child but it died in her arms before the plane landed. The doctor never forgave himself.

Jim and I decided to get married at Fitzroy Crossing because his people were in Perth and mine were in Victoria. It got a bit out of hand because we realised everybody would have to come. Somebody made the wedding dress, someone else lent the car and decorated it. We married in the hospital gardens. I dressed up as a bride with artificial flowers in my hair and in my bouquet. It was October — you couldn't have fresh flowers. Jim wore a tie, white shirt and hands in the pockets. We had the wedding march on record and the piano from the school on the back of a truck just outside the fence for the rest of the music. A girl from Fossil Downs played it. Then we had the reception down at the hotel. The whole town was involved.

HELEN HOLBOROW

Sophie Downs where Helen Holborow lives, is a difficult station to run profitably. Helen's husband, Ray, has to work away from the station a lot. Helen concentrates on making her life with their daughter Lee simple and self sufficient, but at the same time, full and satisfying.

Sophie Downs is a ridiculous shape. From a map, you can see that the other stations were taken up from the good country around it and this is what's left. It's very hilly, just about impossible to muster, even by horse. Someone told me it had been called 'Sophie Ups and Downs' and it's just been shortened. What do we run here? Cattle, horses, donkeys and dingoes. We had the rosy dream that we were going to muster the cattle and sell them like a normal station, but the country is so rough that the cattle walk off any condition going up and down the hills to get feed. We sometimes regret it, but Ray always wanted a place of his own. You get satisfaction from your own place.

The house was here, but fallen down, busted out tin walls, eaten by white ants. We've knocked most of the walls out. At least we can appreciate the view now. It's a very cool house in summer. As you can imagine, the breeze just comes in one end and out the other. It'd be much cooler if we could get a ceiling in.

People complain about the cost of transporting building materials up here, yet just look at all the building materials lying round on the flat.

I feel people conform too much. We like to look at that rock out there. I don't reckon you could see anything better.

When the Depression struck, we had no money behind us. Ray went out with a mining mob. Now he does fencing on other stations. How often he gets home depends on how far from home he is. When he first went out, we didn't have the two-way radio and I didn't have the phone. I wouldn't have known whether he was pinned under a dozer somewhere and he'd think of me, collapsed, broken leg, horrible visitors. The two-way makes such a difference.

I have Lee of course. We have a special sort of relationship. We're here so much by ourselves and she's an only child. I suppose it makes for good and bad. She's terribly independent and grown up for an eight year old.

She spends hours doing things other kids wouldn't be interested in. But it's sometimes hard on her not having other kids to play with.

I'm quite happy to live out here on my own, with a small wardrobe and very few trips south. I don't get lonely, although I get tired of my own company now and then. In our situation, you have to have a very unmaterialistic outlook on life. Ray and I say we never want a fortune, but we'd like to make a little more than we do now, so we could be together.

JANE DE PLEDGE

Like many outback women, Jane de Pledge is alone a lot. She and her husband, Joe, own Mandora Station and a second property near Gascoyne. When Joe is not there, Jane is responsible for the running of Mandora, as well as running the house and teaching the children. But she finds time to brew her own beer, go to the beach and relax.

I met Joey in Perth. I thought Mandora was awful when I first saw it. We lived in a little cottage because Joey's parents were still here. I used to go out on camp with Joey all the time. I think the most difficult thing was living amongst a lot of people — all the staff and the in-laws. There's not much privacy. With a staff, things have to be on time. You can't be in a

bad mood, but they can. I often dream of being here by ourselves, but I
suppose if you didn't see other people you'd go troppo.

There were a lot of blackfellows here when we came, but we stopped
having them when the basic wage came in. You were feeding about thirty
of them for five that could work. With the basic wage, we couldn't afford
to feed aunty, granny and the rest.

I find it terribly hard to send the kids away to boarding school,
especially the girls, because once they're gone, they're gone forever. They
only come home for set holidays and I often feel they have problems that
they're bottling up.

I do get scared when I go to Perth. I feel like a real yahoo, out of touch
with everything. But the only thing I really mind out here is being so far
from our parents. We've always loved them and it's hard not to be there
when they need care.

We're on the Indian Ocean here. The beauty of it, of course, is that
you can go down there and you've got it to yourself. I can't stand it in
Perth, spreading your towel out with 5000 other people. We often go
down on a Sunday afternoon when it's cooling off and have tea down
there. Winter's best for fishing, but we can't do much then, because
we're flat out.

Although it's awful Joey being away a lot, especially when he was
working on the the roads for eighteen months during the drought, I've
developed a lot more confidence, managing on my own. I've had so much
responsibility. Being a wife in the bush, you really feel you're part of
something.

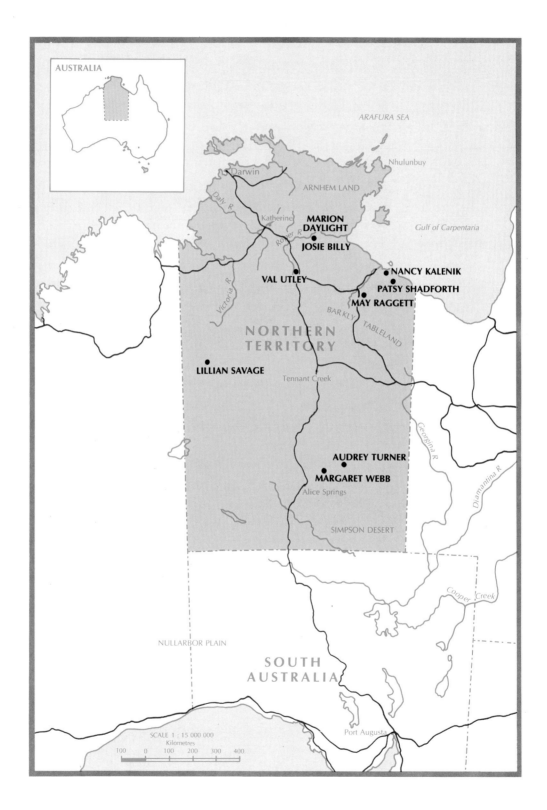

AUSTRALIA

ARAFURA SEA

Nhulunbuy

Darwin

ARNHEM LAND

Daly R.

Katherine

Gulf of Carpentaria

**MARION
DAYLIGHT**

JOSIE BILLY

Roper R.

NANCY KALENIK

VAL UTLEY

PATSY SHADFORTH

MAY RAGGETT

Victoria R.

BARKLY

TABLELAND

NORTHERN
TERRITORY

LILLIAN SAVAGE

Tennant Creek

Georgina R.

AUDREY TURNER

MARGARET WEBB

Alice Springs

Diamantina R.

SIMPSON DESERT

Cooper Creek

NULLARBOR PLAIN

SOUTH
AUSTRALIA

SCALE 1 : 15 000 000
Kilometres
100   0   100   200   300   400

Port Augusta

THE TERRITORY

In spite of the casino at Alice Springs and the growing tourist industry, the Northern Territory is still pioneer country. It is a land of vast cattle stations, with little agriculture. The lives of people in the territory are dominated by the two seasons — the wet and the dry, with many of the rivers flowing only during the wet. One third of the country is semi desert, where the main vegetation is saltbush and spinifex. Much of this country is only just beginning to be developed. Here, isolation is a way of life.

The Gulf country in the Territory is lush, with tropical vegetation and the beautiful Northern Territory ghost gums, with their large, glossy leaves. Big paperbarks grow along the rivers. It is fertile, but hard country to work.

The Northern Territory has a higher proportion of Aboriginals in its population than any other State in Australia. More and more, they are moving off the stations and out of the bush into settlements and towns. The proportion of women in the population is lower than in other parts of Australia and most of the outback women live a life surrounded by men, with little companionship of other women.

ARION DAYLIGHT

Marion Daylight (nee Gulawonga) was too shy to talk much. She was only nineteen and she giggled a lot. She was living in a mustering camp with a group of other women from the Bringung community whose husbands were employed as stockmen by contractor Ned McCord at Roper Valley Station. It is the Gulf country as described in We of the Never Never *and still very much a frontier, with wild cattle that have to be mustered using 'bullcatchers' and helicopters.*

Marion and the other women cook for the men. Flour, tea and beef were provided by the station management. In addition, the women caught fish and turtles, collected bush fruit and sugar bag honey from the native bees. Bush tucker was plentiful. The Roper is one of the rivers in the Territory that flows all year round.

Marion had her baby, Justin, with her on the camp. He was a beautiful, happy child, even though covered with infected mosquito bites and sores common to outback Aboriginal children. Marion was almost coy about the baby, as if she didn't want to make too big a deal about motherhood. In some ways, she was still very much a child herself. She didn't seem to take life seriously and confessed her favourite thing was rock and roll, 'Like them Men at Work', she said.

JOSIE BILLY

Josie Billy lived in the same community as Marion Daylight and was about the same age. She was more serious and mature, but still very shy with outsiders. Josie had been brought up on the Hodgson River Station. Her marriage had been arranged by the tribe and, unfortunately, it wasn't a happy one. She had only been out on the mustering camp once and confessed she found it boring, missing the contact with the larger community back at the station. Nevertheless, she was enjoying the company of the other women and the camp routine.

Much of the time in camp was spent chatting and laughing or cooking bread, damper or meat. All the cooking was done on an open fire or using hot coals for an oven. Although none of the women could explain how they did it, they produced perfectly cooked food. One of the most treasured possessions in the camp was a book on Australian Aboriginals by Laurence Le Guay and Suzanne Falkiner, which the women thumbed through and pored over endlessly.

AUDREY TURNER

Audrey Turner lives on the banks of the Plenty River on Jinka Station. The river runs only after a big rain of 400 mm or so, but the homestead garden, watered by a bore, with its neat kikuyu lawn, is a year round oasis. Although the house and garden are very much Audrey's domain, she loves the country and is an avid birdwatcher.

My husband, John, was born and bred on a station. His father was a pastoralist. I came up here on a trip. I wanted to see Alice Springs, which was then regarded as the real outback. I met my husband and got a job up here with the government. Just after John obtained Jinka, which was virgin land, I came out to the station for a few months to cook in the camp. Eric, my son, was eighteen months old and I was expecting another. There were a mob of wild cattle on this place and John had to clear up the top end. It was a really rugged start to my experiences

because I was a town girl and I wasn't much of a camp cook.

At first, I really resented not having privacy in the camp, but I learnt to make do and the men did understand. I couldn't go without my wash each day, so after dinner, I'd take a basin behind the car, hoping not to be seen and freezing to death with the icy winds. It may have made for a more robust baby, of course. The chappies were pretty rough, but were courteous, not even swearing when I was around. If they did, they'd apologise.

In the mornings, John would say, 'See that white hill, that's where we'll have lunch. Just follow the cattle pads.' I knew nothing about tracking and I used to run up and down the creek banks in the four-wheel drive to find the shallow crossings, not realising how handy a four-wheel drive is. And then I'd lose track of the white hill and John would have to come and fetch me so they'd get their lunch. I'd end up in tears, frustrated and angry.

John built a bough shed first for the stores and then a flash little place using corrugated iron from an abandoned mine. There was only a dirt floor and no electricity, so at least I didn't have to iron.

I'm a bit of a conservationist, not one of those who march, but out here, I'm surrounded by nature. This is my home. I helped make it. A woman out here holds everything together on the home front. You're always there.

AY RAGGETT

As wife of a stockman on Mallapunyah Springs Station, May Raggett lives a life which is becoming less and less common. Increasingly, Aboriginals are opting not to take work that's available on the stations and are moving into the towns. As a result, May lives a fairly isolated life, with occasional, casual contact with the people at the station homestead. She and her family live very simply in a corrugated iron shack with a dirt floor. Her children attend school on the station. Her husband is away a lot, but she's content with her life and proud of him.

My father was head stockman at Cresswell Downs. We had seven children in the family, all girls, no stockmen. My mother died when I was eleven years old and I helped my aunty look after us girls.

I came up to Mallapunyah Springs in 1970 and I married Ronnie Raggett. I meet him already at Cresswell. He came here as jackaroo and he work his way up. My oldest son, he thirteen now, six foot tall. He go to school at Charters Towers.

NANCY KALENIK

Manangoora Station, where Nancy Kalenik lives, is in the spectacular country near the Gulf, with primitive Zamia palms and a tropical climate. Nancy's Yugoslav husband, Charlie, is a fisherman who fishes the Gulf. Nancy lives on the station. She has excellent bush sense and still hunts as well as using food from the station.

I been here twenty-five years. I was born on Vanderlin Island. I was there till I was six, then in the Gulf across the ocean to here. My mum married the owner of this station so we came to live here and this is where I grew up. I only got three brothers. When they went off to school, I stayed here. Borroloola was only a little place then — only the welfare and the store. Most of my people were out on the stations then. Now, they mostly in town. My Dad, he growed up on this station. He worked since he sixteen.

He got the lease on the place. He's my step father. I don't have much
memory of my mother.

We bake our own bread here. We breed the cattle and keep some for
meat. We got goats too and always got them for meat. Sometimes, we got
fish, dugong or turtle. To get them, you go out in the dinghy and just
spear them with the harpoon. When you feel like turtle, you just go out
and get him.

I don't like living in the town. I like it better here, because this is
where I grew up and it's natural here. When my daughter, Rebecca is
older, I put her on School of the Air. We only got the radio here. We
talk to Darwin sometimes.

Wet season here starts January ends about April. So we go into town
by boat, because we can't use the road. Got to go around by the sea and
then come up the McArthur river.

PATSY SHADFORTH

Because of the rough terrain round Seven Emu Station, a lot of the cattle are wild. To Patsy Shadforth and her husband and brothers, mustering wild cattle is all part of a day's work. It is exciting, but often dangerous. The long grass disguises the anthills and holes in the ground which can be fatal for a rider. A big bullock can bring round $500 at the meat works, but given half a chance, it will kill.

Dad's had Seven Emu for thirty-one years. All of us were born out here in the scrub. I remember, we used to run for miles, tailing the nanny goats. There were houses out there, not flash ones, just bark huts. Sometimes, we'd move with the stock camps. We had an aunty and an uncle without any children and we'd go with them a lot.

Uncle Arthur taught most of us to ride. Bull catchers only came in about five or six years ago. Before that, we'd muster by horse. Bull throwing from a horse is a dying art. The boys here know it because they learnt it from Dad. I used to be the only girl out in the stock camp. We couldn't take any tucker that would go rotten after a few days. Mostly took flour, tea, sugar and jam and kill out there and salt it with salt from the pans the next station across. Don't worry about fruit because the bush is full of native fruit trees. Every season, there's a new load of bush tucker. Years ago, you had to be pretty strong, you know, living in isolation. We used to go three or four months out there without seeing anyone. But it's getting much easier now.

The first time I ever went into town, I thought it was very funny. I saw a flush toilet, I pressed the button and ran out screaming, 'Daddy, there's a flood in there.' We had to go to Alice Springs to go to school when I was about eight. There was a whole lot of station kids and we stuck to one another because we understood each other. They used to say the station kids were so quiet, no trouble. We were so lonely the first few weeks, they wouldn't get a word out of us. My brothers and sisters used to cry, but I couldn't. I just wouldn't talk.

I think Mum really carried Dad a lot of the time. Dad had to go away working on other stations for months at a time. I suppose he worked so hard to prove to the welfare people that he could feed, clothe and educate us without help from them. In those days, anybody with coloured blood in them was just taken away and put in foster homes if there was any excuse.

With bull catching, the driver has to be pretty good. He runs over the bull, but not to kill him. Puts the wheel on the shoulder blades to pin him down. The others jump off and tie the legs up, then you winch him in the back of the truck.

My mother was a Yanula. They're coastal people, mainly from them islands out there. They made canoes out of tea tree. My father was a Gwara. Their country's from here to Wollogorang. We lost touch with the corroboree, our people. We lost all that when we went away to boarding school.

VAL UTLEY

A place of their own is the dream of many people who go outback. It's a dream that can take years of work to achieve. Drought, flood, bad prices can all spell disaster. Val Utley and her husband Barry left the lush country of the Atherton Tableland in Queensland to come to the centre to achieve their dream.

When I met Barry he was managing a stud dairy farm at Malanda on the Atherton Tableland. I was nursing and I had no interest in marriage at that time, but I must have been quite interested in him because I got as many cases around there as I could. When we married, we bought a small mixed farm at Tolga and ran that for eight years. We wanted a bigger place. There was an offer of work at Anthony's Lagoon. We had no intention of staying. It was only supposed to be six months work.

We arrived and the manager said to Barry, 'Go down and camp by the big waterhole. You can draw water there.' My youngest was fourteen months at the time, still in nappies, no washing machine. The water wasn't too clean and it was murky because the stock used to drink there. I went up to the homestead and asked if I could have some rainwater for the baby. They said their tank was too low and that if I boiled the water it would be all right.

The six of us lived in a sixteen-foot van and annexe for six months. My husband was building yards and there was no one to help him. I'd help him, sometimes working by lights at night, and I'd teach the children of a day time. But the Territory is a good place for giving you a chance to do well. If you stick with the conditions, you can do better than anywhere else. We were at Anthony's Lagoon for two and a half years and then went fencing and yard building on Tanumbirini Station for four and a half years.

This property, Sunday Creek, we've only developed one tenth of it. There's still a lot of work to go in, but we'll develop it bit by bit. We've

done a lot of culling, so we only have 1500 head of cattle. When my husband first talked about cropping, people thought he'd been in the Territory too long. No one with half a brain would try cropping in this area. Anyway, we started in the wet season of 1977. I helped Barry clear the land with a tractor, getting the trees out and pulling them into heaps to be burnt, helping with the planting and whatever else had to be done. If a woman has a lot of interest in the country, she will survive. Understand the problems and back each other up.

I don't like to say much about this, but when we came here, we had absolutely nothing. I don't think you should be put off by others saying 'That's impossible'. We worked every day for long hours and we managed to do what we thought we could never achieve. A lot of people take holidays for granted and I guess we've missed out on a few. Hopefully, in the near future, we'll be able to sit back a little.

LILLIAN SAVAGE

When Lillian Savage and her husband Bob and their six children arrived at Suplejack Downs, it was virgin country, classified as semi desert. The family have always been as self sufficient and independent as possible. Suplejack Downs is now a working station and the family have bought another property in South Australia.

I left school when I was thirteen. Bob and I used to go to the same school together, lived in the same street. First we had a banana plantation in Broome, but it was blown out by two cyclones. Then we were up at Hooker Creek for three years. Bob was cattle manager there. It's an Aboriginal settlement and in those days everything was good up there and we liked it. Bob was taking a few Aboriginals from Halls Creek down to Yuendumu. They more or less had to make a track through this bit of land and it took his eye and he had a good look on the way back. Anyway, he put in for it. Took a few years, but we got it. Just desert, there was nothing here at all. Nobody had been here, ever.

We came out here in 1965. I've always had faith in Bob. What he sets out to do, he always does well. We like the bush. Our nearest neighbours are at Rabbit Flat — that's eighty-six miles away. The nearest town is

Alice — 480 miles. You don't want to forget the milk.

When we came, we put up a little tent where the garden patch is now. Six children, the littlest only eleven months. There was no wireless, so we couldn't do correspondence. We had to put four of them in St Phillips College in Alice Springs. We got the shed up and then later another little shed. We always had a good garden, plenty of fresh vegetables, chooks for eggs and the goats gave us fresh milk. We were more or less able to live on our own.

That first lot of chooks, we brought in a trailer from Alice. We got stuck in some heavy sand. The only shade was a few big ant hills. The little boys, Robert and William, were with us. It was so hot that we followed the shade round the truck. Took us four days to get out. We always carried a forty-four gallon drum of water with us and Bob was siphoning the water out to take to the fowls and a little bit of a breeze blew up and the hose came out. We lost it all. I shed a few tears. Thought we'd end our lives there. Finally got out by putting everything under the wheel — spinifex, antbed, sticks, and the wire netting off the chook cage. It was great when we made it.

Suplejack is now 15 000 square mile. Used to be 17 000, but then the Aboriginals put in for it and we had to give them an extra bit. It wasn't bordering on anything they had and they aren't doing anything with it. Myself, I feel it's not the Aboriginals, it's the pushers. A couple of the boys that had put in the claim had been in Bob's stock camp. They told us they didn't want it, they wanted us to have it, so we've never really blamed the Aboriginals.

Tell you the truth, everyone thought we were mad when we came out here in the middle of the desert with a lot of little kids. Bob knew he

could show them and I don't want to go anywhere else. I'm not one for parties or a big mob of people. I like meeting people, but as far as dressing up and going out, doesn't worry me. Just a bushie, I guess.

MARGARET WEBB

Injury and premature death are far more common in the outback than in the cities. Much of the work is dangerous Doctors and hospitals are often hundreds of kilometres away. Even the flying doctor can't be instantly available. Most often, it is the men who die and the women who are left to carry on alone, without the support found in the cities. Women like Margaret Webb of Mount Ruddock Station, somehow find the inner resources to carry on with life in the outback.

It was uncanny. The night before Bennett's accident, we'd sat up till two in the morning, looking at the whole program for the property for five years. Bennett had an incredible dream. This station was to be *the* station, he really loved it. The next day, he was killed while mustering. He was driving a bulldozer and hit a gutter and a bull at the same time. The bulldozer flipped over. It was an incredible shock. I didn't realise at the time that you go through a period of six months when you don't even fully comprehend it. But it was automatic for me to feel that I should carry on his plans. I felt as if I'd be letting him down if I didn't.

Bennett and I had shared everything we did — mustering, bookwork, vacuuming the floors, going to town. We relied on each other 100 per cent for friendship. We were loners in that way.

It was incredible that after the accident, everything broke down, it was a nightmare. I was very anxious about the first muster. The first thing was to re-assure the staff that things were going to run as normal. The Aboriginal stockmen had spent two weeks mourning Bennett. The white

bulldozer driver went down to pick them up, but there was no one at the camp. I immediately thought it was because they didn't want to work for a woman. I was sure of it. But what had actually happened was they had gone to town and mourned in their own way by getting thoroughly drunk for two weeks. They had enormous love and respect for my husband. The next day, I thought, we can't wait, we've got to get going. My young

brother, who stayed on after Bennett's death started work with me. I sent another chap down to the Aboriginals' camp.

The chap came back with a grin from ear to ear, because our mainstay, old Archie, had arrived back, very much under the weather and very ill. The workman yelled at him, 'Archie, why aren't you at work?'

'Jingoes, work?' said Archie. 'I thought today Monday.' He was so ashamed, poor Archie.

First thing I realised being a woman is that you don't have the experience working on mechanical things or the physical makeup for some jobs. But I learnt a lot quickly through working in the stockcamp for four months, until I was able to get a good reliable head stockman. I found I was hopeless with mechanical things and I had to delegate to people who specialised in that area. That's how I operate.

My entire motivation comes from my husband's plans and dreams. We had been completely content and when the disaster struck I thought that I could slash my wrists and end it all then. That sort of thing sounds pretty dramatic, but it did go through my head. I'd never had anyone close die — a friend or a relative and for it to be my husband was the ultimate. The only thing was that Bennett had left me so much to live for, so many ideals. There was really no decision to make.

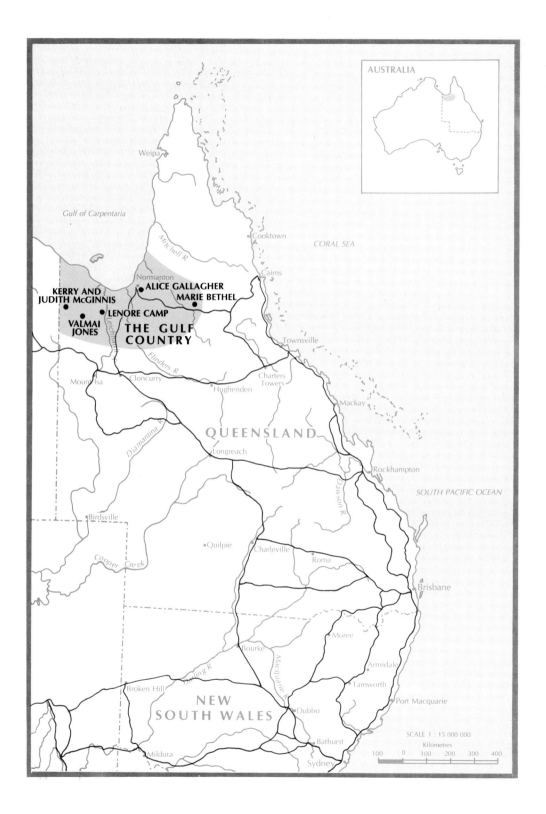

WOMEN OF THE GULF

The Gulf of Carpentaria is low lying country. The shores are fringed with mangroves and the plains are open grasslands, with tree lined rivers. In parts, the density of the scrub makes cattle mustering difficult. The climate is tropical and subject to monsoons. Burketown and Normanton are the major towns, both of which service the stations and attract the growing tourist trade, but both are still very small country towns. Now, drovers no longer take cattle to bigger centres. They either go by rail or road train. But the roads in the area are still poor and as a result, it is very isolated. Women living there are dependent on family and a few neighbours for friendship.

MARIE BETHEL

Marie Bethel runs her property meticulously, but has no great love for it or for her cattle. Her life has disintegrated. Although her sons live on the property, her life has become increasingly isolated. She has no desire to go to town or see people.

My mother, I get me shyness from her. But she was a lady. I'm not. I've always done outside things, mustering, yard mending, fencing, even before Dad died. I enjoyed it and I didn't enjoy it. Always one of those workaholic buggers. Just had to be doing something.

Dad drew this block. He was a young man then, but he'd been to the war. He was gassed there and his lungs were bad.

When Cyclone Agnes came through, there were two little floods, three weeks before. I remember my dad saying, 'You'll never see this again.' My mother got up at six in the morning to see my sick father and I heard her say, 'My God, the water's in the house.' It was knee-deep downstairs. In ten minutes, it rose six foot.

Uncle George got me and Pat out, swimming us out along the clothes line. He stayed down, poking sticks away, he drowned underneath the house. Then the whole house went, just like a boat, for a mile and a half before she broke up. My father got out, but my mother was too petrified. She wouldn't move. They went looking for my mother. Bob Norman dropped us a note. It just said, 'Mrs Aplin's been found', so we thought she was still alive. They carried her body back on a sheet of iron, all the way to Mount Turner. Should have told us the truth — that she was dead. Don't think it strengthened me. Strengthens some, might strengthen you if you're made out of the bloody right stuff.

I only ever had one boyfriend, my husband. We got married in 1956. When we got married, we lived here in an old dump down there — an old, fallen down, one-room turnout. We had no money for repairs and the bloody white ants ate our ports and our pictures. One day, I went through the floor boards. She was white-ant eaten too.

I helped my husband build the place up, just the two of us. Worked beside him. The yards were fallen down, fixed them up. Built yards with a crowbar and shovel. Dig the holes, brace and bit drill the rails. We'd go out and cut the timber with an axe in those days. Most I cut in one day was twenty. That was my limit. I wanted a good place. I used to get a lot of satisfaction, like when I finished a yard or something. I used to like it till a couple of years ago. Now I hate it. I don't even worry about droughts because the cattle are like Chinamen. Two good years and you wouldn't know you lost one.

I shouldn't have been married. If I went away it might have been different. See, my husband was killed a couple of years ago. I don't want to stay here now. I hate this country — the heat, the flies. Another thing I hate about out here, you can't forget anything. Everything you do is death, even the meat you eat.

ALICE GALLAGHER

Alice Gallagher leads a well ordered, comfortable life, on her property, Woodview Station. The patterns of her life have been built up over the years of being a drover's wife and caring for her children. Two of her sons still live with her. She doesn't have labour-saving gadgets and even getting electricity put on hasn't made a big difference to her life. She still prefers a wood stove and a kerosene fridge which is filled at a regular time each week.

I was born in Georgetown and we lived at Crooked Creek. That's twenty-five miles out. I don't remember my father at all. There were seven of us altogether. My mother, she was strong all right. We all used to have to work.

The coach used to come Wednesday and Friday and stay the night. I'd help mother. Sometimes there'd be eight or nine people on that coach, sometimes more. All depends. We had no electricity, no refrigeration. Kept things in a wet bag.

I came down here in August 1929 and I was cooking at the Albion Hotel. My husband, he was a butcher. Had a butcher's shop and used to board at the hotel. His name was James Augustine Gallagher and we got married in 1931. We lived in the town till 1932 then we came out here. He used to go droving. Could be six weeks on the road sometimes and I'd be on my own. I was used to it. The Aboriginals used to be very good them days. Can't trust them these days. My husband had mostly Aboriginals on his team. He'd get them down from the Mitchell River. The drovers would get paid once they'd delivered their cattle to Julia Creek at the railway. Of course, there's not much droving nowadays. Mostly road trains. We still use horses for mustering here.

I never went out with my husband. Had the eight children altogether — six boys and two girls. I had enough to do, looking after the children and around the home. Didn't have power out here then. We had a good wireless though.

During the war, we couldn't have a light on at night, the place had to be in darkness. We had an air raid shelter, rationing, ration tickets, clothing. There was no baker in Normanton. I'd make bread and send it out to whatever station they was on and they'd send it on the mail plane from Cloncurry. At one stage, they thought the Japs had landed. There was a bit of a scare. We were all going to be evacuated, but it didn't happen.

The termites up here they eat palm trees, fruit trees, the house if they could. We planted two palms in 1968. The white ants ate one a couple of years ago. Now we've only got the one.

LENORE CAMP

Floraville Downs Station is on flat, open plains through which the Leichhardt River flows. In the dry, the roads are rough and corrugated. The moment any rain falls, they become sticky and almost impassable. Lenore Camp doesn't see the isolation as a burden. Her strong Christian faith and her sense of humour sustain her in her enjoyment of life.

I first met Walter when I was nursing, but it wasn't a Mills and Boon romance. His sister, Socie, and I had become great friends and I went out to Calvert Hills Station in the Northern Territory, which was his family's property. Mrs Camp was away and Socie and I decided that we'd like to do some cooking. The two Aboriginal kitchen girls used to make sixteen loaves of bread every second day. We thought we'd give them a day off. Don't know what went wrong. Maybe because it was winter, it just didn't rise. Had to chuck all the dough out. Of course we didn't want anyone to see our failure, our huge failure, so we threw it in the garbage bin in the back of the kitchen and carefully put the lid back on top.

When Walter came back we told him we'd been doing some cooking, making some cakes. 'Didn't you make any bread?' he asked.

'Oh no, we didn't make any bread,' we said.

'Better go out the back and take a look,' he said. So we did. There was the rubbish bin, like a big icecream cone and the dough was the blob of icecream. The dough gurgling down the side and creeping along the ground. It had risen! The sun had got in and done the job. Looked like the makings of very fine bread.

When Walter's parents died, we sold Calvert Hills and came over to
Floraville. 'Moving in closer,' people said.

'Closer to what?' you might well ask.

We drove our stock across. It took about ten days, one of the short
trips. I went on a couple of droving trips with Walter, cooking for the
team. I wasn't used to the bush, so naturally, I made a few boo boos. One
particular trip from Calvert to Kajabbi, we were going across the black
soil plain and Walter said he'd meet me up the road for dinner. At dinner
time, I took the wrong road and I looked out over the black soil plains to
see him camped two miles away. Another old drover had come along in a
motor car and Walter and him were talking. I thought I should go over. I
had a brand new Willey's Jeep so I just flew across the black soil plains.
The old drover looked up and saw the Jeep going at all sorts of angles.

'My God, who's that idiot? Fancy coming across the black soil plains.'

Walter was embarrassed and said it just happened to be the cook.
'Typical bloody cook, doesn't know how to look after a motor car.
Wouldn't have half a brain,' said the old drover.

We've had lots of funny experiences with the boys working here. We had a half caste kid, really liked his drink. He'd go into town and come back out when his money was all spent. One time he went in and wasn't back for two weeks. When he came back, I asked him what happened. Thought his money would have run out a good four days ago.

'Oh no Mrs Camp, university people in town, trying to get the Aboriginal language, paying two bob for every new word.' They kept asking him what gender the words were and he didn't have a clue what they were talking about. I asked him how he coped.

'Oh yeah, I sure made something up. After all, another two bob.' So Lord knows how that particular Aboriginal language study turned out.

KERRY AND JUDITH McGINNIS

Kerry and Judy McGinnis were brought up by their father in the bush, travelling around as he went from job to job. They loved the life and with their brother, David, work the family property, Bowthorn Station. It is the second station the family has bought. Yeldham Station was the first. Kerry concentrates on the inside work, while Judy works outside.

Dad was a fitter and turner and had a variety of different jobs. He'd travel round for a company servicing oil rigs and petrol stations. He had worked as a drover until he got his trade and he's done tank sinking, roo shooting and also had a blacksmith's shop at one stage. But he was born in the

bush, was a bushman and we ended up going back to the bush. We came
up to the Gulf in 1962. The whole family were doing droving and
contracting camp work. We bought Yeldham which had no water, no
fences and no stock. Nobody else wanted it. We kept droving and contract
mustering to get together enough to put up fences and put down bores.

When we had two teams, we employed Aboriginal stockmen to make
up the numbers. When we had one, there were enough McGinnises to go
around. Father was always in charge and it went on six years. It was great
fun. The biggest mob we ever had was 2000 but that was a mistake. You
just couldn't handle that number, especially as it was a mixed mob with
breeders, cows and calves. But we didn't have any choice and we could
only do four miles a day. If the results weren't there, you just didn't get
paid. It was a family concern. It would have been different if we'd just
been working for wages.

Before we had any buildings on Yeldham, everything was on the truck.
We'd live out of our swags, there was no time for tarps or tents. It cost
you money if you stopped. Making bread, you'd time it to your stops.

Rise it in the vehicle while you're moving. Knock it down and set it when you get to night camp and cook it in camp. We'd cook bread every day and meat every day. We always had sweets too. Well, you could make rice and custard, vermicelli and custard, tinned fruit and custard, stewed fruit and custard. Rather unusual in the bush. You don't get many camps with sweets every night.

The family unit is even more important today because so many people have lost direction. You've got to have a goal.

KERRY: Some time in 1970, I did senior by correspondence. I was so interested I decided to do uni. I do it through Queensland Uni external program. They're very good, very conscientious. The internal study time for a BA is three years. The way I'm doing it, it'll take me seven, another three to go. But I'm not in any hurry. I do a bit of study all the time, when I can. It depends on the time of year.

JUDY: I'm general station hand. I object to the term jillaroo. Anything that's done on the place, I give a hand with. We're working on a fencing program now, it's a long term job. My brother and I work as a team outside. We've been fencing, dam sinking. There was very little when we came here — basically a tin shed with a concrete floor, no water, no electricity, no bathroom. It was a hurricane lamp job and you carried your water in buckets, no toilet. We had the idea years ago of what we wanted and we were prepared to wait until we could build what we wanted. I don't know how many squares, but it's got fifteen rooms and 9000 bricks. I made twenty bricks a day, in between station work. It's a good way to lose all the skin off your fingers. It took four years to get enough. I made them and David laid them. That's why the walls are crooked.

VALMAI JONES

Valmai Jones revels in the adventure of the bush — breaking a brumby, mustering, swimming in the creek on horseback. Yeldham Station is owned by her father, but it is run as a family affair. It is a big station, but not an easy place to make a living. Valmai looks after her baby daughter, Amanda, but because of the support of her family, also joins in the outside life on the station.

We always thought I was born on the fourteenth till I got my birth certificate to be married and found we'd been a day out. I was born in Mount Isa base hospital and that's where I had my daughter, Amanda.

I was seven when I came to Yeldham. There wasn't much here then — an old tin hut, a stock route bore and another three bores. In the early days, Dad, Leslie and Ian would be out in the fencing camp. Me, Mum, Joanne and Janette were here to look after the bores, the mills, the fences and cattle. Peter was only a little fella. I used to feed the chooks and milk the goats — had about ninety of them. They were really handy when you couldn't get out in the wet to find a killer. But they'd get in and clean up the garden. You couldn't have a garden, so we got rid of them.

I was always involved with the horses. In my spare time, I love playing around with the horses, handling foals or riding up into the hills. We used to try to do school as much as we could, but there was never any strict routine — there couldn't be. When we were mustering, we never did school and then we'd work over the holidays.

I had a brumby poddy foal once called Gidappy. Joanne and I caught him when we were out riding burning fire-breaks. We had a rope, so we chased him and cut him off from the other horses. I didn't have a horn or anything on my saddle. I was just hanging onto the rope with my hands and he pulled me out of the saddle onto my belly in front of him. I had to jump up and tangle the rope round his legs to throw him.

When I was breaking Gidappy, he was really cranky, so I kicked him. If you did something to him, he'd want to do it back to you to get even. He's walking along, his back leg up, trying to kick me back. Another time, had him down at Sandy creek. We decided to go swimming. He was at the top of the bank, so I called him. He'd come when I called him. He came straight down the bank, never seen deep water before, landed in the creek and went in head and all. Talk about wild when he got up, ears back, eyes rolling. I been round horses a lot and they're my favourite animal.

Stephen, my husband, was the bore man over at Lawn Hill and that's where my brother Leslie met him. They came here, so I met him and we started going together. We went back over to Lawn Hill together. I was cooking at the mustering camp there for a while and left to get married back here and haven't been back since. I sort of have continuous company since I was married. I used to be on my own before. Never wanted to go

out — well, there was nothing to go
to as far as I was concerned. It'd be
months at a time before I'd go as far
as Gregory. I used to be made to go.
I'd go brumby hunting when
everybody went out. It's rather
boring for me to be in a town. I've
never been to a disco. I prefer to go
fishing or riding some place.

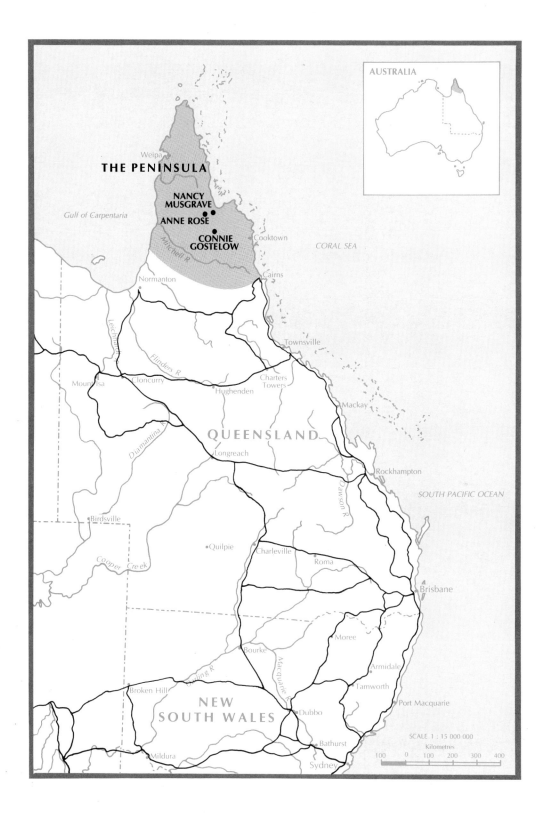

AUSTRALIA

THE PENINSULA

Weipa

NANCY
MUSGRAVE

Gulf of Carpentaria

ANNE ROSE

CONNIE
GOSTELOW

Cooktown

CORAL SEA

Mitchell R.

Normanton

Cairns

Leichhardt

Townsville

Flinders R.

Mount Isa

Cloncurry

Charters
Towers

Hughenden

Mackay

QUEENSLAND

Diamantina R.

Longreach

Dawson R.

Rockhampton

SOUTH PACIFIC OCEAN

Birdsville

Quilpie

Charleville

Cooper Creek

Roma

Brisbane

Moree

Bourke

Armidale

Macquarie R.

Tamworth

Darling R.

Broken Hill

NEW
SOUTH WALES

Port Macquarie

Dubbo

Bathurst

SCALE 1 : 15 000 000

Kilometres

Mildura

100   0   100   200   300   400

Sydney

CAPE YORK PENINSULA

Cape York Peninsula is the isolated, northern-most extremity of Australia. The Peninsula people are conscious of this separation and tend to be clannish, suspicious of outsiders and protective of each other.

There is an enormous range of country on the Peninsula, from the beautiful tea tree forests, teeming with bird life to the coastal plains. Here, the cattle are so wild and the scrub so thick, that they can only be mustered at night, when they come out of the scrub to graze. On nights when the moon is full, the stockmen will rush the mob.

The towns are important as service centres for the stations, but otherwise, they hold little attraction for the people of the Peninsula. They are not easily accessible and the women's lives are, by necessity, centred on the stations.

NANCY MUSGRAVE

Nancy Musgrave, like many other Aboriginals in the area, gets her surname from the station on which she was born. She now lives on a nearby station, Lily Vale, where she is employed cleaning the yard round the house, a task to which she devotes herself with considerable energy and pride.

The area is very beautiful. Electric blue kingfishers dart through the tea tree forests and there are the beautiful pink legged jabiru, brolgas, pelicans and a wealth of other bird life.

I was born at Musgrave Station and we stopped there on that station. When I was a small girl, I play down the river there, playing around. The birds, jabiru red legs, I call them, we got plenty of them up here. We got plenty of bird. See them all around. Sometimes, I'd go fishing, hunting with my mother and father. Little bit of sleeping, little bit of play about.

I got no sister. One die down here when my father been fencing. She

get sick. Die down there at Marina Plain. Long way from the doctor out
here. Now, this time, we got the motor car to get to doctor, not like
before.

I married there at Musgrave. I lost the one little one. My husband, Joe,
he teach me how to ride. He was a stockman, me and him, all rushing
round the camp. I used to go out mustering with my husband. Oh, yeah,
it was a good life, this one, mustering in the bush out there. Sometimes, I
fall from the horse.

I been here a long time with Mrs Shepherd. I work here, help feed the
racehorses, give them a hand to clean up the yard. I clean everything,
keep them clean. That's my job.

My husband, he die now. He died and I lost him in Laura. My brother,
he tracker in Laura. He work with the policemen. Yeah, Georgie
Musgrave. I can track, get bush tucker, get yam. Yeah, on holiday it good
to go out find sugar bag, anything.

I think about all our relations, how they die. Think about it sitting
down here. Lost my husband in Laura. I worry about it at first, now I
don't think about it. Don't think about nothing now. Poor old fellows.

NNE ROSE

*The Rose family have moved around a lot, but Anne adjusts by keeping
family life central and maintaining a sense of humour. Her husband,
John, manages Violet Vale Station and Anne not only accepts but
actually enjoys the isolation.*

When Dad came up round Mareeba in 1932, he bought land and grew
tobacco. We didn't have any of the highfalutin machinery that's around
now. When the plants were ready, we children — my brother and I —
would take them out to the peat field and drop the plants and Mum and
Dad would put them in the ground. We'd water them with a little tin
from a tank that Dad filled up from the creek. The next morning, we'd
get up as early as we could and cover them with paper until they were
strong enough to stand the sunlight.

Jack and Newells, the grocery store, were marvellous with credit.
Tobacco farmers had only one pay cheque a year, when they sold the

crop. Jack and Newells stood by them all that year. When Mum and Dad first came up, Errol Flynn was working on a tobacco farm. He was a bit of a larrikin even in those days. Had a fair booking up, like the rest of the farmers and workers. When he went to America and became famous, Jack and Newells wrote and asked him if he'd kindly pay his bill. He sent them back an autographed photograph.

John and I have been married eighteen years. From that resulted four cheeky kids, none of whom we'd give away. We don't care if they live with us till they're fifty.

In 1977 we went out to manage a little property at Bilwon. It was on the other side of the Baron River and when we wanted to go into town, we had to cross the river in a little dinghy. You'd go across all dressed up with the three little ones, gingerly step out the other side, bucket in hand, because you had to wash your feet and dry them and then put your stockings and shoes on, to be respectable to go into town. I used to say to John, 'Jackie Onassis wouldn't know she's living. I wonder what she's doing today.'

When we left Bilwon, we went to manage the Sundowner Horse Riding Park. We used to get a lot of tourists and when things were busy, John would get young Anthony to go with him because he's full of cheek and something to say. One day they were out with some Americans and came across some quinine berry trees. This American lady said, 'Anthony, what are these things growing on this here tree?'

'Bush strawberries,' he said.

'Can you eat them?' she asked.

'Oh yeah, you can eat them,' said Anthony. She took a great big mouthful and of course her face just twisted up and froze. I mean they're just so bitter.

'Anthony, you little son of a bitch,' she said.

We've been up here fourteen months now. I wouldn't care how far out we were. I feel we're not far enough yet. Goodness, the last time I went to Cairns was almost a year ago. I couldn't be bothered bumping up and down that road.

I saw a friend up at Musgrave Homestead a couple of weeks ago. They were listening to the ABC's *Always on a Sunday*. The fellow was doing an interview about the Peninsula and this chap says, 'Up there it's uninhabited, nobody lives there.' My friend's young son jumped up and down and cried. 'Mum, you write to them and tell them people do live here. We're people!'

CONNIE GOSTELOW

Connie Gostelow's shopping list, pinned to her back door, has all the usual groceries needed by any household, but it also has reminders for things such as five rolls of barbed wire. Connie uses the barbed wire when she goes out mustering to string around trees to keep the horses confined at night. Connie is known throughout the district as a great horsewoman and is very knowledgeable about stock.

From the time we could sit up, Dad put us on horses. He died when I was about thirteen and Mum put us right the way through school. We went down to Mareeba for about six months and I went to school there. It was great to have friends, someone to play with. Then we came back up to Palmerville, where my uncle was. He'd been in partnership with my father. Mostly, it was just my uncle and me doing the mustering.

I married Miles in Cairns and came up to Koolburra. There was no house, only a little shed. Miles and all the men used to go away mustering. The shed had a roof and three sides — used to leak like a sieve when it rained. After I had Anne, I'd be having to shift the cot all the time. We had no vehicle, only a horse. It was our only transport. It didn't worry me until we had the baby. I had no way of getting anywhere if anything did go wrong, no telephone, no radio. The only way to get anywhere was the horse. Luckily, nothing did happen.

The men seem to go away and leave the women. They think, 'Oh well, they can cope.' A woman is more likely to cope than a man if he's left behind on his own. A lot of men wouldn't be out here if we weren't out here too.

1960, they started putting the house up and it was finished by the time Kenny was born. Had a bit of comfort then. But I'd been used to it rough. Mum had never had electricity or any mod cons.

I go all the time with the mustering camp. The year Kenny left school, there were only Miles and I, Kenny and one nephew. There were only four of us for those years when money was short and we couldn't afford to pay the darkies' wages. One year in particular, all we lived on was bread, corn beef and rice. That's all we could have. So we battled on as best we could. It was a family-type thing. We didn't have folk on big wages and that's what got us through.

Now, if we're going out into the wild country we'll get a few extra men to help throw the bulls. I've tangled with them at different times. I try to stay away from them as much as possible. Too right, they're fast. If they come at you, you just get going as fast as you can. The best way, if you can, is to ride into the mob, because they won't go into the mob.

We shoot the brumbies if we see them, but with the young foals, we keep them and poddy them. We've had about seven now and they turn out real quiet, good horses.

Out here, I like the quietness, the freedom. You can go where you want with no one hassling you or bustling you. Koolburra's 615 square miles so you're not looking behind you to see who's following you or expecting someone to run over you. Sometimes, I think it'd be all right to get a small place, somewhere where there's better country, but then there are other things. You know, it'd upset you, you'd be too close to towns.

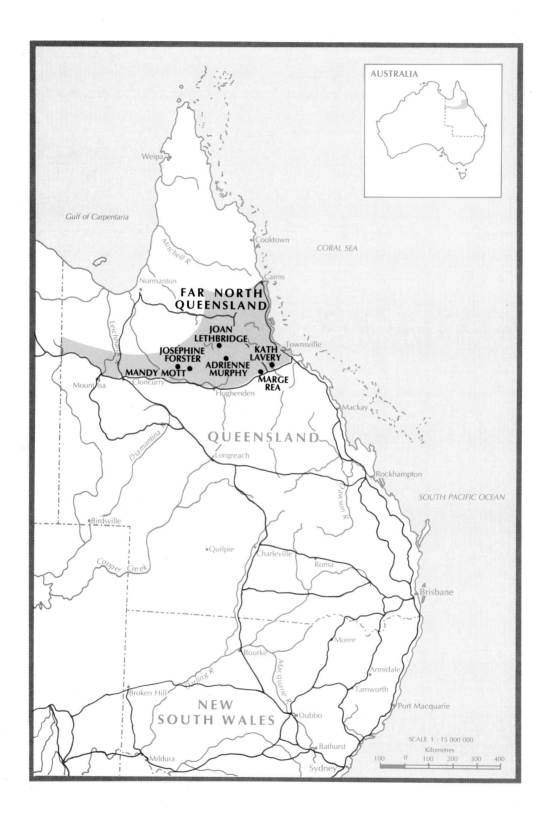

AUSTRALIA

Weipa

Gulf of Carpentaria

Mitchell R.

Cooktown

CORAL SEA

Normanton

Cairns

**FAR NORTH
QUEENSLAND**

Leichhardt

**JOAN
LETHBRIDGE**
•

Townsville

**JOSEPHINE
FORSTER**
•

**KATH
LAVERY**
•

MANDY MOTT
•

**ADRIENNE
MURPHY**
•

**MARGE
REA**
•

Mount Isa

Cloncurry

Hughenden

Mackay

QUEENSLAND

Diamantina

Longreach

Rockhampton

SOUTH PACIFIC OCEAN

Dawson R.

Birdsville

Cooper Creek

Quilpie

Charleville

Roma

Brisbane

Moree

Darling R.

Macquarie R.

Broken Hill

**NEW
SOUTH WALES**

Tamworth

Armidale

Port Macquarie

Bourke

Dubbo

SCALE 1 : 15 000 000

Kilometres

100   0   100   200   300   400

Mildura

Bathurst

Sydney

FAR NORTH QUEENSLAND

Charters Towers, an old mining town, was once the centre of the richest gold fields in Australia. It is now much smaller, but still a very pretty town. The surrounding countryside is undulating, covered in eucalyptus and scrub. Many of the properties around Charters are small and overstocking has destroyed some of the vegetation. Further west, the properties are bigger and the country flatter, with great grassy plains stretching into the distance.

K ATH LAVERY

Most outback women have to be physically energetic. Their life requires much more physical activity and there are far fewer labour saving devices than in the city. Physical activity becomes a life long habit, which in some women, such as Kath Lavery, seems to create boundless energy.

My first husband was a man from the bush, involved in all the things I was. He'd worked in mines and on stations before I met him. Nothing more I can tell about him, only that we had four children before he died. Then I sold everything out there at Broughton and moved into Charters Towers. I was a widow for a few years, vowing never to marry again. But I'd known Edwin a long time. He was droving and it was natural that we married. He drove cattle for lots of stations before we ever bought this place.

I used to take the groceries out to him, taking my baby Anne. It was no difficulty to take your children. You'd just get organised, plenty of food, plenty of water and make sure it was a nice comfortable camp. We'd be up at dawn and they'd wake up as comfortable as a four room home.

We had a little block of country, ten miles of it. Now, we've got forty-five. We'd camp out there and go mustering, all the children, Edwin and I. I'd carry Anne in front of me on the horse. That sort of thing was no effort then, although I wouldn't like to be doing it now of course. In times of hardship it's sheer strength keeps you up. It's not brains, it's the will to go on, a love for your cattle.

Once we were bringing the cattle back from agistment, a very hot day, everyone was thirsty. Edwin asked for the quart pot, scooped some up and downed it. He passed me one and I looked into it. 'I wouldn't drink that,' I told him, 'It's full of tadpoles.'

'I thought I felt something go down my throat,' he said.

I love going out amongst the stock. I'm getting on in years, but they can't hold me down. I still ride and muster with the best of them. I'm not skitting, but it's better than rotting away in a rocking chair.

MARGE REA

The outback is still, very much, male territory. Some women feel the lack of female companionship terribly, others adjust more easily. For many, like Marge Rea, it is a real liberation being able to give full rein to the boisterous, tomboy side of their personalities.

When Bruce and I came out here, there was an old miner's house, from the town. They number every board before they pull them down and then they put them up together again.

We've got cattle and horses here and we're very involved in camp drafting. I'm secretary of the Stock Horse Society for Charters Towers area and also the Northern State Management Council. Bruce has always camp drafted. He believes you breed your own. We've got an Australian Stockhorse stallion that came from New South Wales. You break them and do the whole lot. If any of the horses are hurt, I do the patching up. My dad used to do that at a time there weren't many vets around. If

anyone had a horse or a dog that got
hurt, Dad stitched them up.

The underground water here is all
salty, so we have to pump our water
from a bore three miles away. White
ants eat holes in the pipe
periodically. One time, Bruce and I
got back from a long trip. It was
about eight at night and there was
no water. We went out and tried to
start the pump, but we couldn't. So
we gathered up our towels and soap
and a couple of buckets and went
down to the bore that waters the
cattle. I threw a bucket of water over
him and he threw one over me and
then proceeded to tell me how I'd
have missed all this if I'd married a
townie. He always says I'd go mad if
I couldn't dig my toes in the dirt.

When the boys were little, we still
owed a lot on the place. Bruce
couldn't put a lot of time in, so I
taught the boys to ride, to drive and
to swim. My boys can look after
themselves. They can do their own
washing. It might mean a bit of mud
goes into the machine, but I've
always worked on the theory that we
haven't got any relatives around and
if anything happened to me, I wanted
the boys to be able to look after
themselves. See, if a town kid gets
into a bit of a spot, he can always
throw his clothes into an automatic
laundry or a dry cleaner's. A
country kid can't do that.

J OSEPHINE FORSTER

The ultimate in creativity for countrywomen is often seen as cake or jam making for the local show. Resources in the outback for any artistic endeavour are pitifully small. Jo Forster has artistic sensitivity and talent. Against the odds, she has developed her talents and now, through teaching, nurtures it in others.

I went nursing because I felt there was no opening in those days to earn a living art-wise, not for a girl. I must say the nursing's been very useful out here — everything from delivering a dark girl's baby to fixing a parrot with a chest problem.

When I married John, there was more social life here. Undoubtedly the pioneers worked hard, but they had staff. Now, families tend to do their own work and go out and work on other properties. Some of the young ones even go shooting roos, which we used to think was a terrible thing, or form shearing teams.

Our first house was a solid little house with a tin verandah roof. We used to fry. We didn't have much money at first, so the first thing we got was a radiogram because we figured you could sit on it, eat off it, listen to it and dance to it.

In 1972, Mervyn Moriarty brought art education out here. He learnt to fly and started up a school. He was an idealist, he cared. He was poor and would wear Vincent de Paul clothes. He even left here one year knowing he had nowhere to go. I'm forever in his debt. Because I got so much help from him, I feel I have to help others. I started teaching art because Mervyn Moriarty suggested I do so. People need it so much out here. There is nothing cultural, just hard work.

When things get bad, you don't collapse in a heap and moan and groan. Happiness doesn't come from material things. We've had the beef slump, the wool slump, the droughts and the fires. To me, they aren't tragedies, they're setbacks. A tragedy is the real thing, when you've had a son who's been killed. Our son Gregg died. Stephen, our youngest, had been alerted that he'd have to come home from school, but he didn't know the reason. 'What's happened?' he asked. 'Did the house burn down?'

I said that I wished it had.

It made me realise you can't live in fear. You go through trauma and you deal with it. Fear is a waste of time. Before Gregg died, I used to worry if the boys were late home. It makes you unable to live wholesomely and happily because of being so afraid of what has happened, what might happen. I always tell my students to leave their egos and fears in their cars.

 # ANDY MOTT

Mandy Mott is Jo Forster's neighbour and their love of art brings them together. Mandy is also very involved in the station life of Somerville and works hard both outside and inside.

I was brought up in the Brisbane Valley. There, fifteen miles to town was a long way. That's the distance to the boundary here and I think nothing of just running out there.

After school, I did primary training in Toowoomba, then went to Sydney. My grandmother had offered me art lessons and I wanted to do them in her lifetime. I met Tony at college and came up here in the holidays. I just loved it. We'd work hard, but we relaxed in the evenings with meals under the stars. One Christmas I went up to Esmeralda, another of the Mott's properties. I camped with the men and it was stinking hot, about 113 degrees. I used to wear a sarong in the evening

and Mr Mott used to say I lifted the standard of camp dress.

When I married Tony, I knew I also married his way of life. He was born up here and it's in him. We arrived up here just before Christmas and on Christmas Day we were out feeding molasses licks and pulled five head of cattle out of the bore drains. We had to shoot them, then we poisoned them as Christmas cheer for the piglets. We worked non stop that time in the drought, daylight to dark, trying to save stock. It's wretched to see your livelihood slipping through your fingers.

I worked with the men all day from six in the morning, plus feeding them in the evening. Tony originally thought you should offer the men something more than work, a lifestyle as well. So they ate with us, but it just didn't work. They didn't feel comfortable. They have their way of doing things, you have yours. They are really happier to have their meals apart.

We have machines that replace what people did in my in-laws' days. They used to have a cowboy — gardener, a couple of house gins and a cook. They were people, somebody else around. Once I had three dogs and thirteen pigs and I talked to them for ten days. Sometimes I feel being on my own because I'm the only female here.

The fact that the environment is so harsh has definitely made me more feminine. It's a reaction to wanting to be treated as a female. Everything is against you in being feminine. It would be easy to chuck it in, not make the effort.

My husband is with the men all day. That could really make me feel like an outsider. Tony says that it's a man's world, but a woman has her place out here. What you have to offer as a woman is really important out here. Even the workmen appreciate it. They don't say so, but they do.

ADRIENNE MURPHY

Gregory Springs is a family property and this, in part, explains Adrienne Murphy's attachment to it. The old family homestead is slab construction and surrounded by a beautiful garden, easily watered because of a spring on the property. Adrienne works outside with the men all day. Much of her work involves horses and cattle.

I've lived most of my life on Gregory Springs, except for boarding school and after that when I got an office job in Sydney for twelve months. When I left that, I didn't want to go back to the city. We've all come back here, one by one.

When the muster's on, I'm one of the team. I don't say I do the work of a man. I don't think many women can say that they totally take the place of a man because we don't have the physical strength and, mostly, we're not as brave if there's wild cattle or horses to be handled.

We've always used horses here. We have only done two little helicopter musters on a very small part of the place where it's rougher country and the cattle are wilder.

In the 1982 drought, we had nineteen poddy calves at one stage. We had what we called a 'calfeteria', a board on the fence with holes for the teats to be stuck through. They learn pretty quick to come up for their milk. I got rather attached to them of course. I think I'm lucky to have been brought up in the bush. I love the life and the animals — it's not that you don't work hard.

I imagine I wouldn't be so interested in the country life if I was working for someone else. When it's your own, you don't have to stick to weekly routines. If there's something you want to go to, you can just go if the mustering allows or if you're not in the middle of a howling drought. You don't have to wait till Saturday or Sunday. You might work weekends, but you're more free.

I can go without seeing other people for a certain time, but it's nice to get away. We get away now a lot more than we did. There are several race meetings I go to during the year. I don't see my old school friends very often. Most of them are married with children.

Women look after their kids, worry about meals and washing. I like working with the men. I feel I can have a joke with them because I've been sharing their activities outside. I would say I can relate to men on the land, rather than women, but none of us are indispensable.

JOAN LETHBRIDGE

Glenmore Station is mainly open eucalypt forest, beautiful, but very remote. No major roads service the area and most of the roads are still dirt. Joan Lethbridge's surroundings seem very masculine but she retains a feminine sensitivity to the environment.

My father's father took up this land and passed it on to his sons — my father and my uncle. Dad, Mum and us kids came out here and pioneered Glenmore. There was nothing, bar a well on the bank of the creek. No fencing, no house. Dad built a house on the banks of the creek, laid on water to our camp. That's where Mum was, with four kids, no help, no Toyotas. In dry times, there was no taking licks and hay out. Dad had a beautiful black horse called Comet and he'd ride out to check the waters. He'd be gone about a week and Mum and us would be here alone.

I'm not married. When I was younger I thought it'd be nice to have a mate. Put my head on his shoulder and have a good cry. I've got over that. You learn to live with yourself. You have to.

Knowing what my parents did here makes my feelings for Glenmore even stronger. Mum taught us correspondence until we went to boarding school. Unfortunately, I got very ill and couldn't finish my education. I left school very young and I've been here ever since. I love the stock and the bush, even though you take the bumps. You see how dry it is, but then you see the beauty in the flush of the season. I'm not talking financially. We make a comfortable living, we don't splash our money around. We keep putting in improvements. Three hundred square miles of country takes a lot of improving.

During mustering, when the country's green and the cattle are fat, you do work hard. But it's not like when you've got the drought. That's a lot more strain psychologically. 1982 was a bad year. My brother John and I decided to burn a break because we were worried about fires. We dropped a few matches and the fire went out that night — or so we thought.

The next morning we were out mustering, the big smoke went up. Johnny told me to ride back to camp and see that everything was safe. I got up to the ridge where we were mustering and I could see the situation was pretty grave. Put my horse into a full gallop, got to the camp, there was the fire coming down with a good south-easterly behind it. Pulled the saddle off and left it on the bank of the dam and let the horse go. Bundled the four swags, transceiver radio and anything else I could into the back of the Toyota and drove it onto some cleared ground. Reefed the tents into the dam. I had to drag the tucker boxes. They were too heavy to lift and the fire was getting real close. I was getting a bit blown about. By the time Johnny got there, I'd had it with shock. When my other brother, Lux, got there with the cattle, it was all over, smoke rising from burning logs. He couldn't see any gear. It did have its humorous side, when I heard that boy say, 'Holy hell, the bloody lot's gone.'

One of the most wonderful experiences in the bush is when you've slogged out a long dry, keeping the cattle alive and the first storm breaks. Big wool packs will come up, then fizzle out. Heart breaking heat storms, cattle killers we call them, because they make the cattle walk. Cattle will go fifteen miles or so, looking for a storm. Smell it, get there to nothing and they've got to make it back to water. You wait and you get the good fella. You wake up and hear a rumble of thunder. Look out, hello, what's on now? You can see the big fellas, the wool packs, the lightning. You look for chain lightning running from the ground up to the clouds. Then it's hullo, this is it, she's breaking this time.

In the flashes of lightning you can see the rain wall. Then you get the wind, smell the wind, smell the rain. The gullies start to run. If you're a bushman, and lived all your life in the bush you can smell the torrent in the gullies. Hullo, she's running a gully, a good one, a drought breaker. It's coming closer and closer and you're praying like hell it'll come, right over the top. Sure enough, it's right on course. By that time, everyone's out there barracking. You think you'd better go inside, but you can't. The rain comes — the smell of it on dry grass — it's absolutely beautiful.

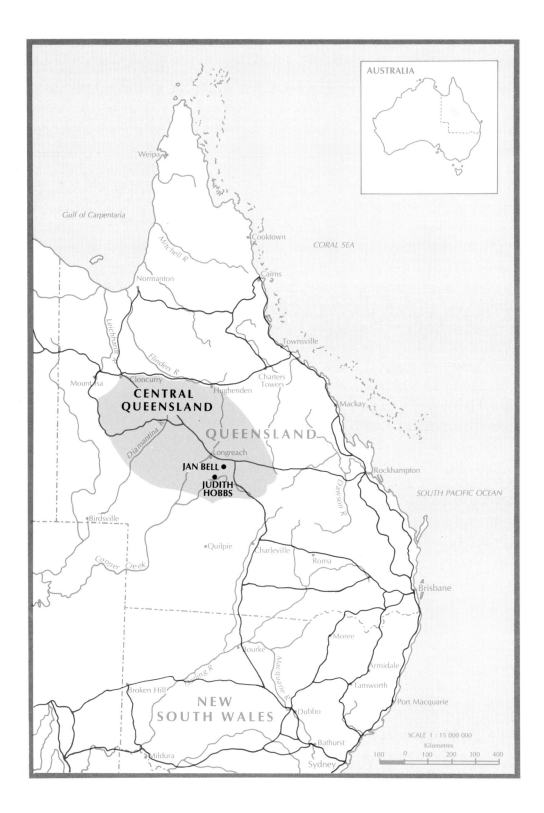

AUSTRALIA

Gulf of Carpentaria

Weipa

Mitchell R.

CORAL SEA

Cooktown

Normanton

Cairns

Townsville

Leichhardt R.

Flinders R.

Mount Isa

Cloncurry

Charters
Towers

Hughenden

CENTRAL
QUEENSLAND

Mackay

QUEENSLAND

Diamantina R.

Longreach

JAN BELL ●

Rockhampton

JUDITH
HOBBS

Dawson R.

SOUTH PACIFIC OCEAN

Birdsville

Quilpie

Charleville

Roma

Cooper Creek

Brisbane

Moree

Bourke

Armidale

Macquarie R.

Tamworth

Port Macquarie

Broken Hill

Darling R.

NEW
SOUTH WALES

Dubbo

Mildura

Bathurst

Sydney

SCALE 1 : 15 000 000
Kilometres
100   0   100   200   300   400

CENTRAL QUEENSLAND

The country around Longreach is flat scrub country, much of it Gidgee country. The Gidgee is a small acacia, with an unpleasant smelling flower. In times of high humidity, it becomes all pervasive. The properties in Central Queensland are big and run mainly sheep. It is an area that is famous for its shearers and abounds with shearing legends.

JUDITH HOBBS

During the annual Winton to Longreach Endurance Ride, which attracts the best bush riders from all over Australia, Judith Hobbs makes a gourmet breakfast at the stopover at Maneroo. The fact that some of the riders barely notice what they're eating doesn't worry her. Judith enjoys style and refinement for its own sake.

When I was young, I had the most dreadful fear of dairy cows. I'd stay with my grandfather during school holidays and his cows used to chase me up the road. Now I'm chasing cattle round the yard and my grandfather's probably up there laughing at me. Most of my eighteen years at Birkdale, I've been working on an artificial insemination (AI) program of the cattle, mustering, branding and keeping the books.

In 1972 we introduced Charolais cattle. Our poll Herefords were all artificially inseminated and produced cross Charolais calves. I designed the numbering system for our Charolais stud cattle. Because of our AI program, we were practically the first people in the district to number our herd and to put them into books. That's how we developed our stud. We couldn't afford to get anyone to do it for us, so we had to do it ourselves. From growing up, terrified of cows, now, I'm making them.

Now, we've got television and the telephones are becoming more reliable. I like the lifestyle, but I'd like some sort of security so we don't go up and down financially so dramatically. It's wearing on lives and marriages out here, this boom and bust. It's insane the way we have too much money one minute and nothing the next. The wool depression, the cattle depression and now the big drought we've just had.

I think the advantages of the lifestyle outweigh the disadvantages. Of course people out here choose to have all sorts of different lifestyles. I think it's important to keep standards high. That's why we always dress for dinner and have proper silver service at the table. A lot of people don't, but we do. It's more comfortable, isn't it?

Loneliness is something you make yourself. However, I am a lonely sort of person. Henry keeps me going. He spends more time indoors as he gets older, not going out to work in the yards and things. He keeps my self image going. That's what usually motivates a woman, husband and image, isn't it?

Henry has been described as being one of nature's gentlemen and he is, right through to his bones, a gentleman. Even though he's on crutches and I'm helping him along, he never goes through a doorway in front of me.

I love being here at Birkdale. I love being Mrs Henry Hobbs, a beloved second wife. There was a beloved first wife too, you know. He's used to loving his wives.

JAN BELL

Dandaraga is run as a family concern, with Jan, her husband David and their two grown-up children all working the property. It is primarily a sheep property with a few cattle, but in addition, the Bells are as self sufficient as possible, with a vegetable garden and chooks and a general philosophy of making do.

One of the best things about living in the country is that you don't have to do anything to suit other people. You work at your own speed and you're governed by the amount of daylight, the seasons, the rain — or the lack thereof. I think you have to be pretty resilient in some ways. In the drought, your husband's out there all day with dying stock and you're dealing with it too. Early in my marriage, I couldn't take it — I was too emotionally involved in things dying. I had to toughen myself. To me, to be involved is the whole thing. Some women are only involved as far as the garden fence. A lot of property owner's wives see their role as a social one and as home-makers. Good for them, but that's not for me I'm afraid.

I was determined I wouldn't fall apart when the children went to boarding school. I enjoy being involved in the running of the place and I appreciate my husband's attitude to this. Perhaps it might be a good thing for a husband to have a wife who's only interested in inside things. Then there's no confrontation. There's always some confrontation where a wife works with her husband. And if everybody works outside, they should all muck in when you come inside. I have the happy situation where David says 'Everybody get their own'.

Men are becoming less discriminatory, but there are still a few who find it difficult to accept women in the traditional male fields. But with the shortage of employees, men are coming to accept that women are part and parcel of their work.

Quite recently, I've started birdwatching again. A few years ago the Royal Australasian Ornithological Union did a survey of all Australian birds. I read about it and thought it's something I could be doing as there wasn't anyone else in the district doing it. I took part in the program and that started me off seriously watching birds and becoming aware of birds in the area. I took my binoculars every time I went anywhere and noted any new bird.

I like cattle and I thoroughly look forward to the cattle work that is done twice annually. We don't have ticks here so we're very lucky.

When we were first married, we weren't living here at Dandaraga. David would have given his eye teeth to have it, but it didn't appeal to me because it was Gidgee country. The Gidgee smells to high heaven when it flowers. I found the desert country much more attractive, although it is less so financially. But since we've moved to Dandaraga, it's come to mean everything, it's my lifeblood. I'd be heartbroken if, for financial reasons or some other reason, we had to sell. I'd be devastated.

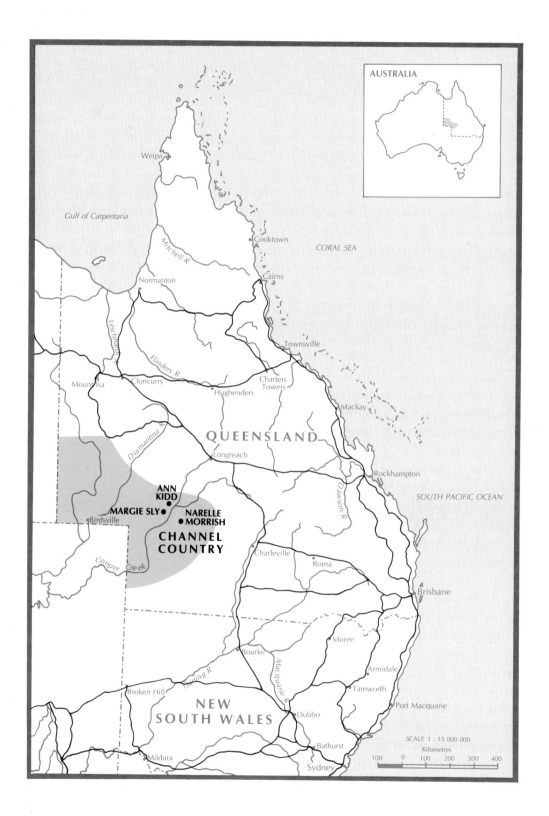

AUSTRALIA

Gulf of Carpentaria

Weipa

Mitchell R

Normanton

Leichhardt

Flinders R

Mount Isa
Cloncurry

Hughenden

Cooktown

CORAL SEA

Cairns

Townsville

Charters
Towers

Mackay

QUEENSLAND

Diamantina R

Longreach

ANN
KIDD

MARGIE SLY

Birdsville

NARELLE
MORRISH

CHANNEL
COUNTRY

Cooper Creek

Rockhampton

SOUTH PACIFIC OCEAN

Dawson R

Charleville

Roma

Brisbane

Moree

Bourke

Macquarie R

Darling R

Armidale

Tamworth

Port Macquarie

Broken Hill

NEW
SOUTH WALES

Dubbo

Bathurst

Mildura

Sydney

SCALE 1 : 15 000 000

Kilometres

100   0   100   200   300   400

CHANNEL COUNTRY

South west Queensland, or the Channel Country, as it is known, is well supplied with rivers — the Bulloo, the Mulligan, the Georgina, the Thomson, the Barcoo and others. Because the country is so flat, when there is more rain than usual, the country almost invariably floods. Water spreads across the vast flat plains, drowning livestock and submerging homesteads. Before the rains, the country is dry and desolate, with huge sandhills. Afterwards, it is covered in yellow and white everlasting daisies and other flowers. It is mainly sheep country but after the rain is the best beef fattening country in the world.

ARGIE SLY

Margie Sly spent her early childhood on a station, eating bush food and living a life in many ways similar to that of her tribal ancestors. She has adjusted to a very different life in the town of Windorah. Windorah is very much a frontier town, servicing the surrounding stations. Unlike many outback towns, there is little racial tension in the town and there's a good feeling between blacks and whites.

I really come from the Maree Track. I was born on Mulka Station, Maree. I like it out there, people are friendly, but not as friendly as here though.

My mother couldn't read or write. Learned by her parents, the wild way. In those days, they couldn't do what we do now. You know, they were sort of under the Acts. So that they couldn't spend their own money. They had to go to the police station and just get their government ration and all that, get their clothes from there. I reckon we're free now,

get our own money and buy anything we want. But they couldn't do those things, so it was pretty hard.

Yeah, my mother, she knowed everything, been reared up out in the bush getting wild tucker. She showed us what ones to eat and what ones not to eat, berries and things like that. I enjoy living out in the country, like the wild food out here. Wild fruit and mulga apples. We go out and get them. They grow on the mulga tree. Little round green things, real sweet, grow along the road there. We like kangaroos and emus and wild turkey sometimes.

After Mulka Station, then we come down to Birdsville. I went to school and got married there. I worked on the stations, housemaid down Tara Station, went from there to Mount Leonard Station. The women, they was good, everywhere I went to.

My husband was a grader driver, he died of cancer, good while ago now. Now, I live with another bloke. He works on the council at Jundah, drives a truck. He helps me. I got nine children now. Mornings, I keep really busy. I got the same old thing to do over and over. The afternoons, I got nothing, sit round and fight with the kids, go little walks. Sometimes, she gets real hot and can't get no vehicle to go down the river to swim. Mosquitoes are bad.

I had the house twelve month now. Our regional fellow got it for me. We pay rent on it. We go to each other's place, have meetings, department meetings, you know, for these houses, whatever we want. If we need anything here, like I wanted a hot water system here, we have a meeting. We let it go through, then it comes. I go next door to the meetings. They got the secretary, treasurer and all. We write our own cheques. They got a cheque book and we pay anybody who do work for us around here. Like repairing things — as long as it go through the meeting first.

Kids don't give me a chance to be lonely — always fighting or crying or calling out. The men have to go to work and then we have to cop the lot, like cutting the wood. Oh, then I like to go over to the pub and have a cold Four X beer.

NN KIDD

The Kidd family are well known in the Channel Country, with extensive properties in the area. However, in spite of the family wealth, Ann Kidd, her husband, Sandy, and their children live simply in a casual country style at Little Dell Station. The family are strong Catholics and in many ways, Ann is a typical, strong, stoic bush mother.

I came out here to nurse Sandy's grandmother. I arrived in the 1963 floods and I can remember we flew over Adavale, which was submerged in water, with people stranded on the hotel roof. I first met Sandy when I stepped off the DC3 here. I remember my first impression: 'Humph, who's that funny little fellow?' Sandy used to meet every plane that came in and he'd give them a hand fuelling up, so that's how he happened to be there.

Sandy's mother and father picked me up in the four-wheel drive and took me over to Mayfield. In those days, every Sunday night there were pictures at Mayfield on the lawn in summer and, on cooler nights, in the room with the louvres around. A lot of the locals came along — it was quite a social event.

I couldn't get over how friendly everyone was. Coming from the city where I'd always had to call anyone older 'Miss' or 'Mister' or at least 'Aunty' or 'Uncle', I had expected it to be 'Yes Miss Kidd, no Miss Kidd.' But it was all Bub, Kitty and Lily. Old Grandma Kidd was a marvellous old woman. When I was with her during the day, I started asking questions about Sandy and she'd give me gen on him. I was only there six weeks before we were engaged.

Some women aren't cut out for it out here. I don't know what it is because you can't really say it's lonely, or isolated — well not that isolated. Country women do a lot of work and I think that's why we are a lot happier. If you've got physical things to do, things aren't going through your head, like stress. But I can't stand housework. I hate it. When you're working with sheep or cattle you feel like you're getting somewhere. When you've done it, it's finished for a while. Housework's there all the time.

Communication is a problem. We do have a phone, but the exchange is only open certain hours and there are certain times you really need it *now*. But there's been a lot of progress since I came. The only bitumen then was a bit in town. And in 1963, they started on the road over the channels. Now it's bitumen all the way to Brisbane, bar the twenty kilometres Charleville to Quilpie. They've got an electricity generator in town and the water's been upgraded. A man used to have to go and

pump it from an old windmill. It's made a real difference to the gardens in town.

Every spring out here we get flowers. Now, because of the winter rain, we've got a greater variety. The flowers make such a terrific contrast from what it was before.

ARELLE MORRISH

Narelle Morrish has, at times, a hard life and a very isolated life. Women not born and bred in the outback make enormous sacrifices to adjust to their husband's lifestyle. The oil rig on Springfield provided Narelle with companionship and friends. When they pulled out after a disastrous air accident in 1983, she was again alone much of the time as her husband, Bob, was working away from the station. However, she has some pleasures — books and a record player with a splendid record collection.

I didn't really want to go on the land, Bob wanted to. He'd been reared on the land, spent most of his life on a property, so it had a great pull on him.

I went nursing before I got married because I was very religious. I felt that the most important thing in life was helping others, but as I grew older I realised there was more to life than just that. In the first year, I discovered nuns weren't really special creatures, they had moments of bitchiness, just like the rest of us. And then I discovered men.

A mate is terribly important. I think anyone living in the bush by themselves must be crazy. It's not terribly important to me where I am — it's more important who's around. We moved here three and a half years ago, knowing it didn't have a house. If we'd had generous seasons, it wouldn't have mattered because we could have built something fairly quickly, something less primitive. Once the drought came, we had to borrow another large amount of money to send the cattle back on agistment, so the chances of building were nil. Basically, all we've been able to do is keep cattle and horses alive.

That sounds like a sad sob story, but it isn't really. People make a choice about what they want to do. If they're not happy they won't stay. Even though it's so primitive, we enjoy the lifestyle and see improvement in the long term. Otherwise, we wouldn't be here.

We live in the engine room. A neighbour and Bob extended it and put a gauze partition onto it which we use for sleeping. It's not weather proof, but you don't get bothered by rain very often, not in a drought. And you feel guilty when you whinge.

Country women who are discriminated against by men often see it as their role in life. A lot of them aren't given equal ownership of property or cattle and a lot of them wouldn't want to be hassled with it anyway. I don't think country women have a tougher life than city women. It's like the Robyn Archer record we've got, *Ladies choice*, where she talks about neurotic suburbia, the housewife who has everything. Husband takes off for work in the morning and she's left in the flat. What more could she want, with the digital watch, radio and television? Gives the children a big dose of aspirin to make them sleep. It's a good rubbish.

Bob works for the Department of Primary Industry in Charleville, so I've been here alone a lot. I've been spoilt having the oil rig. They were

drilling a mile away, over the creek, so I'd see someone every day and it'd give me a very secure feeling. I thrived on the companionship, meeting people from different areas, with different attitudes and upbringings. They're leaving now, after the tragedy. The accident was hard to take, believe it, cruel. It made me realise how temporary we are, that life isn't forever. Unfortunately, we spend most of the time just doing the basics. We get bogged down instead of really living.

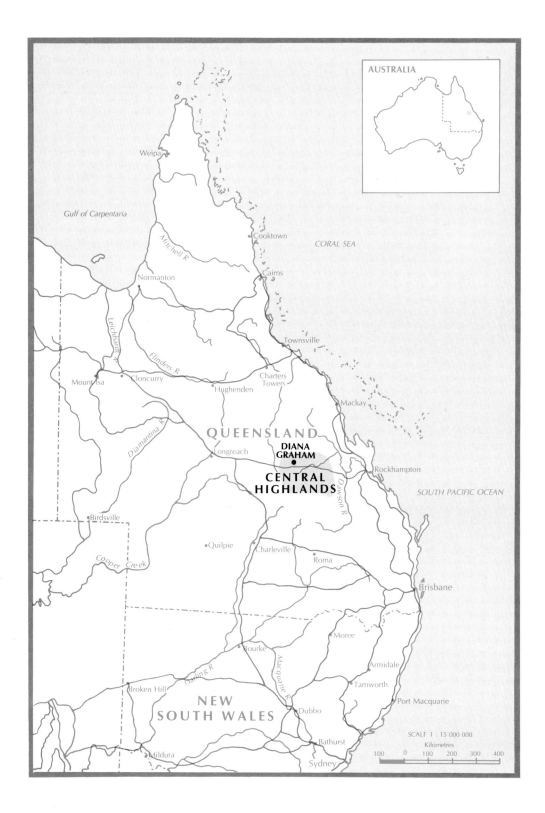

CENTRAL HIGHLANDS

DIANA GRAHAM

The mountainous, timbered country around Withersfield, the Graham family property, has a romantic feel, with its wild cattle and little mountain streams. Here, the country dictates that horses are used for mustering. Diana Graham is a passionate horsewoman, an English woman who has fallen in love with life on an Australian station.

My parents lived about fifty miles from Oxford. Like a lot of country people do in England, they hunted to occupy their days. I was very keen on hunting. I started when I was about two. By the time I left school, my life revolved around hunting. But I felt it was a way of life that was disappearing, that sooner or later one would have to do without that sort of life. So I was interested to come somewhere where horses were still a way of life and a necessity. I came here when I was twenty-four and I travelled round quite a few stations. I'd been given Johnny's address and eventually rang him up to say I was coming and jumped on a bus which arrived at two in the morning. I thought I couldn't possibly get the poor man up — I didn't know if he was nineteen or forty. Fortunately, he was there waiting. I couldn't believe I was so fortunate as to be picked up by such an attractive looking man and that it was Johnny.

The next day we went out to the back country to muster some wild cattle. It was an awful muster because there'd been eight inches of rain. We depend on being able to trap the cattle at waterholes, but with the rain, the cattle were in small mobs and very difficult to handle.

Johnny had a contract to repair some yards so we went out cutting trees. I was terribly keen to impress him, so I got busy with a big hammer barking the iron bark posts. It was all too much for him, this English girl who could bark posts.

When I married Johnny, I went everywhere with him and we did everything together. For the first four months of pregnancy, I carried on mustering and cooked for the men. After that, I had to give up riding. I only expected to have one baby and I imagined I'd drag this poor unfortunate child around with me on the horse and that would be that. When I was told it was probably twins, I had this vision of holding two small things with wobbly heads. In fact, that was exactly what it was like, an absolute horror story for the first few months.

The first time we camped out with them, they were about six weeks old. I'd forgotten all those things like ants running everywhere and the fact that we'd just burnt that bit of country and it was black everywhere. The next time, we were mustering and I was cooking for the men in the camp. I'd bath the babies in a bucket. One of the men got very indignant because he filled his water bag from the bucket, took a drink and said, 'Oh dear, this is disgusting.'

I said, 'I think you've just drunk the babies' bath water.' I couldn't stop giggling and he was just so cross.

I get desperately lonely here if I'm not out with Johnny. Johnny works pretty well seven days a week, so our whole life revolves around Withersfield. If I didn't have an interest in it, I'd have a very boring and unsatisfying life. I could take up embroidery, I suppose.

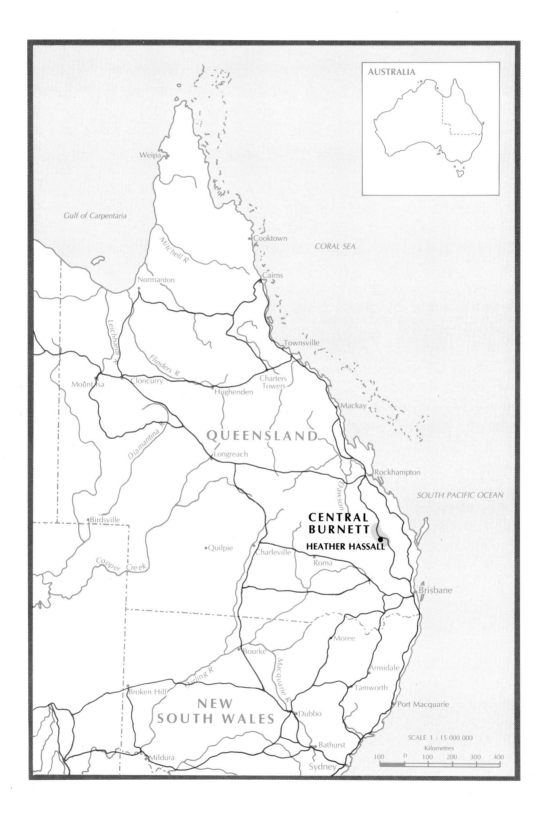

AUSTRALIA

Gulf of Carpentaria

Weipa

CORAL SEA

Cooktown

Mitchell R

Normanton

Cairns

Leichhardt

Townsville

Flinders R

Mount Isa

Cloncurry

Charters
Towers

Hughenden

Mackay

QUEENSLAND

Diamantina

Longreach

Rockhampton

SOUTH PACIFIC OCEAN

Dawson R

Birdsville

CENTRAL
BURNETT

HEATHER HASSALL

Quilpie

Charleville

Roma

Cooper Creek

Brisbane

Moree

Bourke

Darling R

Macquarie R

Armidale

Tamworth

Broken Hill

Port Macquarie

NEW
SOUTH WALES

Dubbo

SCALE 1 : 15 000 000

Kilometres

100   0   100   200   300   400

Bathurst

Mildura

Sydney

CENTRAL BURNETT

The Central Burnett is beef and dairy country. When there are good rains, the native grasses spring up to provide lush feed. In the dry, the country becomes sunburnt, dry and parched looking. In recent years with the ability to irrigate it has become a famous citrus growing district.

HEATHER HASSALL

Deraby Station, where Heather Hassall lives, now has many things people in the city take for granted — the phone, a mail service and electricity. There is now a sealed road into the town of Mundubbera. Heather has lived through the years of transition from isolation to an environment in which she is more in touch with the outside world.

I was born in Bundaberg and went to boarding school at a very early age because it was difficult to get good governesses. I finished my schooling at NEGGS, Armidale, where there were lots of girls from properties and we were able to ride, which gave us a link with our former lives. On my father's side of the family, we had some people who'd made a success of writing — Aldous and Julian Huxley and Alexander Browne (Rolf Boldrewood) who wrote *Robbery under Arms*. I had a hint of it in my blood. *Only* a hint, I'm afraid, but I fancied journalism. I was, I believe, the first person in Australia to write advertisements in doggerel verse. I wrote a piece for J.B. Chandler and Co to advertise their Radiola:

ODE TO THE RADIOLA

Once country life was termed as slow,
to city folk, a farce.
They spoke of bushies with a smile,
and called us green as grass.
The press reporters waved their pens,
they printed jokes galore,
with 'woop woop' as the butt of mirth,
to make the people roar.
Depicting really mental scenes
of harmless country bumpkins,
with figures lank and faces blank,
all innocent as pumpkins.
The country cousins would confess,
that rural life was slow,
but like a bombshell in their lives,
there burst the radio.

Now all country homes are filled
with bright and happy beams,
A rival to the ancient sun,
Marconi's wonder gleams.
The bush resounds with sounds of jazz,
affairs of state and song,
and orators with lusty voice,
give speeches loud and long.
Curlews which once claimed the night,
are wondering what is wrong.
So rally round and buy a set,
that's extra good and strong.
Down the street called Adelaide,
in Brisbane, bowl along.
To find the set we recommend
to Chandlers you must go
and to your daily prayers you'll add,
'God bless the radio.'

My father became ill and I kept writing for Chandlers at home on Monduran Station and, at the same time, assisted the men outside. My husband was so much older than me, that for a long time there, we had no interest in each other. I was a child to him. But our families always visited and later on, we discovered we were both interested in reading. We discussed books and there was always plenty to talk about. We married in 1935.

At first, we only had one mail service a week. It came by buggy, very slow. To have fresh bread, you made your own. Also butter, soap, all that kind of thing.

On the weekend, we'd play tennis with our neighbours, have parties and so forth. We had two sons and they'd often have friends home from school. On special occasions, we'd take all the furniture out of the loungeroom, get a band in and have a dance party. There were a lot of people then who played for dances. I remember one particular station master who had a beautiful voice and would entertain us with singing. We managed to scrape up a jazz band too, not first rate, but most enjoyable.